U AND NON-U
REVISITED

U AND NON-U
REVISITED

Edited by Richard Buckle

DRAWINGS BY
TIMOTHY JAQUES

DEBRETT'S PEERAGE LIMITED

THE VIKING PRESS · NEW YORK

To Holly

One night in New York last May I was told dinner would be late because the English television serial *Upstairs, Downstairs,* was showing. This was introduced by Alistair Cooke, who had the hard task of explaining why English servants had not murdered their masters long before the latter were killed in the 1914-18 War.

I told my host that I was fed up with this serial because every time I dined with Felicity, my nearest Wiltshire neighbour, it always seemed to be the night of *Upstairs, Downstairs,* and she too changed all the household arrangements because she could not bear to miss a moment of it. I added that Felicity's former husband Anthony was now married to Pauline the daughter of Hermione, whose sister Angela (now dead) played the part of the cook in the popular serial. Furthermore, I told him, the girl-friend of Anthony's and Felicity's son Henry, *i.e.* you, was the stepdaughter of Alistair Cooke. He had ceased to listen.

When Brookie (of Debrett's), whom I had met through Felicity, Henry and you, asked me to edit this collection of essays, I thought he must have been overwhelmed by my genius. Not at all: he was simply inviting me on your recommendation. That is why I dedicate this book, with my love, to you.

June 1978   DICKY

P.S. When I first met Hermione, Henry's stepmother's mother, she was entertaining the troops in Naples in 1944; and we had dinner after the show with Peter Rodd, the husband of Nancy Mitford.

Contents

Acknowledgements

Mr Brooks-Baker wishes to thank Robert and Elizabeth Darley-Doran and Robert Jarman for help with his article. Sir Iain Moncreiffe thanks his wife for devoting herself to a day-long session of typing in order to catch the post from Scotland to Wiltshire, which nevertheless took five days (express), because of the increasing English mania for bank holidays.

*   *   *

The editor, Richard Buckle, thanks Mr H. B. Brooks-Baker for employing him, and his brilliant friends for rallying round. Sir Iain Moncreiffe is his oldest friend (1940) among the contributors, Lord Harewood (1948) his closest, and Sir Cecil Beaton (1946) the one he sees most of, as he is a neighbour in the country. Mr Christopher Sykes, before he moved to Dorset, used to live even nearer, and when Richard Buckle bought his cottage, Christopher and Camilla Sykes constantly put him up, fed him, and helped him to settle in. Mr Sykes is the only contributor – apart from Professor Ross – who also wrote for *Noblesse Oblige*.

Mr Patrick Montague-Smith is a new and wonderfully helpful friend. Lady Mosley, Professor Ross and Mr Philip Howard, however, the editor yet awaits the honour of meeting. The two last were indefatigable in correspondence.

The editor had hoped to include something by a life peer, but the new *noblesse* did not oblige. Richard Buckle's greatest grief, though, was that Sir John Betjeman was unable to collaborate, but he thanks him for his funny letters and for having given him joy for nearly fifty years, and sends him his love.

The genealogical trees, begun so blithely, were carried through under the expert supervision of Mr Patrick Montague-Smith and Sir Iain Moncreiffe.

The editor thanks Mr Tim Jaques who submitted to incessant nagging over the illustrations and travelled to Wiltshire to 'finalize' certain points. He thanks Mrs Anthony Harriss not only for typing and retyping, but for criticism and for ferrying copy and proofs to and fro' between him and the press at Tisbury.

Lady Daubeny encouraged Richard Buckle during the book's early stages. She and Lady Harewood put him up when he went to London for discussions. Count and Countess Alexander Schouvaloff made various suggestions and proposed the subject of at least one illustration. Lord Pembroke confirmed the editor in his subversive theory about the spread of 'Double-U'. Miss Astrid Zydower, the sculptor, was staying with Richard Buckle when Timothy Jaques was doing his drawings, and one or two of her comments proved acceptable to the long-suffering illustrator. All these friends have earned the editor's gratitude.

Richard Buckle is grateful to his mother for waiting on him hand and foot after an operation; to Mrs Thomas Chambers for so patiently doing his shopping; and to his kind drivers Gerry and Maureen Bone, without whom work on the rushed production of this book would have been held up.

Foreword

H. B. BROOKS-BAKER

MANAGING DIRECTOR DEBRETT'S PEERAGE

Are the English the most snobbish people in the world? Why have the English upper classes evolved a system which enables even a foreigner to detect whether an Englishman is socially acceptable or not, simply by his choice of words or his accent? Although these two questions are frequently asked by people all over the world, in my opinion England is among the least snobbish and class-conscious countries. Far less so than America, for example, which basks in the reputation of being the most democratic of nations. However, this does not mean that snobbishness is rare in England. On the contrary, it is prevalent to some degree in most areas of society; and the peculiar characteristics of language and behaviour which come naturally to the English upper-classes and are often imitated in vain by the middle-classes are dealt with in some detail below.

Until recently, and to a certain extent even today, any family in the Southern states of America whose position and land were acquired after the War of 1861 was generally regarded as being beyond the pale. Yankees refer to this as the 'Civil War', while southerners would consider it bad form to call it anything other than the 'War Between the States'. When I was living in the South as a child, a French nobleman arrived to visit the plantations in our area. Being a planter himself, he was conversant with every aspect of farming life, and the people who were involved in it. Two of the largest plantations he visited were owned by a Colonel C., who was descended from a pre-war family, and by Mr B., who belonged to a post-war family. Shortly after he had surveyed Mr B.'s plantation, the Frenchman attended a luncheon at Colonel C.'s antebellum house, to which all the leaders of local society had been summoned. In the course of conversation, he expressed his enthusiasm at the new methods of farm production Mr B. had introduced. Colonel C. agreed that his neighbour's technological methods were indeed superior to his own, but added that one should not, of course, take this too seriously, since 'ol' Mr B is a self-made man'. 'That must have saved God a lot of trouble', was the Frenchman's response. Although I was only twelve at the time, this devastating observation made its impression.

This type of American 'colonial' snobbishness is not rare, even today, and it is much more severe and unyielding than its English equivalent. People of many different origins can be found to have established themselves in English society. The Astor family, for example, arrived in England from Germany via America relatively recently, for the first of that name was naturalized in 1899, but they are now fully integrated into the English social scene. Members of noble English families, and this, of course, includes those of Scotland, Ireland and Wales, have frequently married French, South American, German, Belgian, Jewish, southern American, and even Yankee wives, as the following list of twenty examples, which go back no further than the 1930s, will show:

Denmark: Birgitte (*née* Henriksen), Duchess of Gloucester
America: Pamela (*née* Colin), Lady Harlech
America: Virginia Fortune (*née* Ryan), Countess of Airlie
India: Clara Evelyn (*née* Wadia), Countess of Strafford
China: Hsiao Li (*née* Wen Chi), Lady Lindsay of Birker

'a self-made man'

Yugoslavia: Stanka (*née* Losanitch), Countess of Lauderdale

France: Nicole (*née* Schneider), Duchess of Bedford

France: Athenaïs (*née* de Mortemart), former Countess of Rosslyn

France: Jacqueline (*née* Gelpi), Lady Kenilworth

Finland: Helena (*née* Backstrom), Viscountess Margesson

Belgium: Pamela (*née* Chimay), Marchioness of Hertford

Belgium: Régine (*née* d'Ordorp), Lady Rodney

Hungary: Judith (*née* Marffy-Mantuano), former Countess of Listowel

Germany: Irene (*née* Harrach), late Lady Howard de Walden

Holland: Elizabeth (*née* van Swinderen), Lady Inchyra

Italy: Cristina (*née* Casati), late Countess of Huntingdon

Spain: Maria (Mima) (*née* Alvarez-Builla y Alvera), Countess of Iddesleigh

Austria: Ottilie (*née* Losch), late Countess of Carnarvon

Norway: Anna (*née* Sommerfelt), Lady Congleton

Philippines: Luthgarda (*née* Fernandez), former Lady Moynihan

Every craft, profession and trade is also represented in the inner circles of English society, which is not the case in most countries. In Silver Jubilee year, a 10-year-old French girl who was given an elaborate birthday party in London was told that she must do her best to look chic, because not only had several royal relations been invited, but her socially prominent Sainsbury cousins (owners of a chain of food stores) would also be present. So astonished was the girl at the idea of inviting commercial people to her party that she asked her mother whether it would not be a good idea to invite the Safeways and the Fortnum and Masons while they were about it.

In reality the Belgians, the French, the Americans, the Austrians, the Germans, the Italians and the Spanish, in that order, are the leaders of twentieth century snobbishness. What, then, has created the U and non-U system* that Nancy Mitford and Professor Ross revealed to the world a quarter of a century ago? As we have seen, anyone, provided that he is liked and appreciated, can be absorbed into English society, but this made it inevitable for a secret system to be evolved which separated those who were initiated from those who were not, *i.e.* the masses. It has long been my contention that the English U and non-U system, which so subtly divides people into social groups, was necessary because the majority of English people are very similar in looks and temperament. (However, one must accept the fact that the Nordic type is not the only one encountered in the British Isles.) Frances Hodgson Burnett's *Little Lord Fauntleroy* is a story that could only be Anglo-Saxon, for the blonde-haired, blue-eyed son of one of the wicked Earl's tenant farmers might easily be exchanged for the Earl's grandson in England. This would not happen in most continental countries, where the difference in appearance between the children of a peasant and those of an aristocrat is so startling that one could easily conclude they come from two entirely different races.

George Bernard Shaw explained in *Pygmalion* how the inadvertent use of one incorrect word can reveal an intruder into society, and Evelyn Waugh observed that every upstart wants to draw the line immediately below himself. The fashions of U and non-U were gradually evolved by those who thought along snobbish lines in the early fifteenth century, when French passed out of common use and English began to be spoken by people of all classes. Historically speaking it is not very long since the nobility began to send their children to schools where they learned Latin and Greek, instead of having them tutored in these languages at home. Through the knowledge of Latin lay

* U means upper class, non-U means not upper class

the path to Church and State, while the mastery of Greek opened the door to intellectual pursuits. The Latin pronunciation taught at public schools, particularly at Eton, was so peculiar that at the Congress of Berlin in 1878 the English delegates were able to use it among themselves as a secret language. It would certainly have been considered non-U for them to have spoken Latin in any other way.

Being U not only means that one speaks with the right accent, but it also means that a person must choose the right word or phrase. The list of acceptable and unacceptable words that follows this Foreword shows the pitfalls that await the unwary who have not yet been admitted into the inner circles of English society. The book itself will further illustrate how these words should and should not be used. Although the choice of words and accent is vitally important, clothes, clubs, vocations and hobbies are also U and non U, as well as such things as the way in which a person walks. A bouncy walk is just as non-U as a rapid scuttle. Furthermore, it is even claimed by certain reliable authorities that it is distinctly non-U to be uncircumcised.

From the time that U children are very small, they are subtly conscious that they are members of the élite. This was most eloquently demonstrated by the nine-year-old Daisy Ashford in her charming book, *The Young Visiters*. At one point she disapprovingly described the 'jellus' Mr Salteena as being 'flustered with his forks' and unable to cope with his finger bowl.

In his trialogue with the philologist Professor Ross and with Philip Howard, the distinguished correspondent of *The Times*, Richard Buckle introduces a new dimension to U and non-U, and coins the term 'Double-U', to describe the parodying of lower class slang by members of the upper classes, who can frequently be heard using such words as 'pong' for 'smell', 'scoff' for 'food', or 'flog' for 'sell'. Mr Howard, who has written a series of scholarly articles on the misuse, or over-use of certain modern words in the English language, has shown how the incorrect use of such words is unattractive, and therefore non-U. He observed that this was particularly true in the over-use of technological terms in everyday speech. A U person never uses words that are longer, or more complicated than necessary. If Nancy Mitford were with us today, she would undoubtedly agree that a statement like, 'As of this moment in time, it was deemed necessary to escalate before finalizing ...' was not only ugly, but definitely non-U.

Here is another refinement. An Englishman who is *afraid* of appearing non-U would never dream of placing his knife and fork at the end of a course anywhere but in the middle of the plate. The knife would be on the right and the fork on the left, the prongs towards the centre of the table. One who was certain of his acceptance in society would do just as he pleased, for he would be unconcerned by what was 'done' or 'not done'.

Lady Mosley objected to the idea of her sister, Nancy Mitford, writing on the subject of U and non-U twenty-two years ago, because she feared that it would cause harmful controversy, and lead to new friction between the classes. However, she has kindly agreed to write a brief chapter for this book, for even though she deplores snobbery, she does realize the sociological and historical value of her sister's observations. In *Noblesse Oblige,* the witty Nancy Mitford dragged out an ancient skeleton from the cupboard, and enabled us to study – and even be amused by – a subject that had hitherto, by tacit consent, been considered unmentionable. *U and Non-U Revisited* examines the changes that have taken place in the U and non-U syndrome during the last quarter century.

A Beginner's Glossary of Non-U Words and Their U Equivalents

Non-U	U
binding	constipating
bye-bye (or ta-ta)	goodbye
cereal	cornflakes (shredded wheat, Alpen, etc.)
classy	smart
commence (to)	begin (to)
corsets	stays
costly	expensive
cycle	bicycle
dandruff	scurf
dentures	false teeth
dress-suit	dinner jacket
escort	male companion
expecting	pregnant
gift	present
give me a tinkle	ring me
greens	cabbage (or other leaf vegetable)
handbag	bag
home (a lovely)	house (a lovely)
horse-riding, or horseback riding	riding
ice-cream	ice
I couldn't say	I don't know
ill (he has just been – *i.e.* vomited)	sick (he has just been). See 'sick', below
jack (in cards)	knave
lady	woman
lounge	drawing-room
mantelpiece*	chimneypiece
mirror*	looking-glass
notepaper	writing paper

pain (to)	hurt (to)
pardon?	what?
pass on (to)	die (to)
pastry	cake
perfume	scent
perspire (to)	sweat (to)
phone	telephone
portion	helping
postage stamp	stamp
preserve	jam
raincoat	mackintosh
recollect (I don't)	remember (I don't)
reposition (to)	move (to)
Royals	Royalties
Scotch	whisky
Scottish*	Scotch
serviette	napkin
settee	sofa
sick (in bed)	ill
soiled	dirty, dusty
the States	America
sufficient	enough
sweet	pudding
toilet	lavatory, loo
toilet paper	lavatory paper
town (in)	London (in)
unpleasant odour	awful smell
wealthy	rich
wire	telegram

* Sir Iain Moncreiffe maintains that to say 'Scotch' for 'Scottish' or to call the words 'mirror' and 'mantelpiece' non-U is pure Mitfordism.

American Section

Non-U	U
affair	party
beautician	hairdresser
chaise lounge	*chaise longue*
charming	sweet
company	dinner guests
couch	sofa
cravat	tie
cute	attractive
drapes	curtains
entrée	meat course
folding stuff	money
folks	parents or relations
high school (when it refers to a private school)	private school (American – what would be a public school in England)
hose	stockings
the Law	the Police
limo	limousine
maître D (pronounced Dee)	*maître d'hôtel*
nice girl	virgin
old man	father
old lady (or woman)	mother
real (*e.g.* a real good time)	really or very
top drawer	socially or economically important
trousers	pants
tux	tuxedo
home	house
hostess gown	evening dress worn at home

'Maître D!'

Nancy Obliged

THE HONOURABLE LADY MOSLEY
(DIANA MITFORD)

I believe my sister Nancy Mitford got into the 'U' business by mistake. She had an article to write for *Encounter*, the subject was aristocracy. When she had said
everything she could think of the article was still much
too short; in those days there was nothing as amusing as
honours lists *now* to comment on. While she was pon-
dering how best to pad it out, Professor Ross sent her
his interesting thesis about the use of language, and
after asking his permission to do so she put it all in. It
fascinated the public and the newspapers and *Encounter* sold out in no time at all. For a few days Nancy's
interpretation of Professor Ross's research pushed
murders and rapes on to the back pages. Perhaps I
exaggerate, but it certainly got a lot of publicity in un-
expected places.

What she had written also made quite a few people
cross, which was fatal with somebody like Nancy who
enjoyed nothing so much as teasing. When she realized
it had annoyed she was naturally overjoyed, and entered
into the spirit of the thing, collaborating in a book
called *Noblesse Oblige*. In the long run perhaps she
wished she had thought of something else to put in
Encounter, because she preferred to be known as a
novelist and a biographer rather than as an expert on
etiquette or whatever it was.

The whole affair seemed to me at the time, and seems
to me still, quite silly and unimportant; not Professor

Ross's work on language, but the way it was blown up and exploited. It is a mistake to erect unnecessary and imaginary new barriers in England, where there is a certain amount of rather absurd 'class' feeling which should be encouraged to wither away. In fact, it is withering away, and 1956, the year of *Noblesse Oblige,* seems a very long time ago. The generation which has grown up since then would laugh at all these arbitrary and fiddling little rules.

There are certainly fashions in words and expressions, and fashions in accents, but they have very little to do with 'class'. Within one family differences can be noted. My grandmother pronounced all her a's short, her a's in 'France' and 'dance' were like ours in 'ash' or 'can'. She pronounced 'Gloucester' 'Glawster', while we said 'Gloster'. She never sought to impose her pronunciation upon us, or told us that her way was right and our way wrong. Similarly my grandchildren are inclined to laugh because I pronounce 'offer' 'orfer'. Neither they nor I would assert that one way is correct and the other incorrect.

People now say 'absolutely' when they mean 'yes', and 'this is it' when they mean 'that's the point'; those under thirty-five pronounce 'room' 'rume'. Are they being 'U' or not? It seems completely irrelevant.

The English language, spoken all over the world, constantly evolves and absorbs new words, or gives new meanings to old words. Expressions often come from America. I like the way Americans use the word 'great'. When they say of some dogsbody 'So and so is great', it is very nice, and when they comment on some plan like a luncheon invitation, 'Yes, that will be great.' Occasionally one hears an American murmur 'Great, great,' to himself apropos of nothing at all. This might catch on in England; if it does, will it be accepted by these experts, or not? Does anybody care?

[2]

In future there can be no argument about the accents and expressions used by individuals, because what they say has been recorded. We know that Bernard Shaw had an Irish accent, and that the Duke of Windsor spoke 'mid-Atlantic'. How intensely interesting it would be to hear Frederick the Great's French, and his German; to have a record of Shakespeare's voice, or Queen Elizabeth's, or Julius Caesar's; to discover whether Napoleon spoke French with an Italian accent. Biographers of twentieth-century characters can hear their subjects' voices, and their choice of words, both of which are important and revealing.

When my autobiography was published in 1977 an American journalist, Alistair Forbes, gave it a very bad review in *The Spectator*. Nobody likes bad reviews, but this one was entitled 'The only non-U Mitford book', which, as far as I was concerned, more than made up for the text.

Snakes and Ladders

A DIALOGUE WITH SIR CECIL BEATON

BUCKLE You wrote once of your 'ambition to break out of the anonymity of a nice, ordinary, middle-class family', and in 1923 'I am an insufferable snob' . . .

BEATON Yes, I always felt there were thrilling people just round the corner whom I never managed to meet.

BUCKLE To quote the diary of your years at the university: 'I wish I could find the really best people in Cambridge.'

BEATON My only outlet seemed to be the dramatic clubs, theatricals.

BUCKLE You wore rather peculiar clothes –

BEATON Red or gold ties, gauntlet gloves, Oxford bags –

BUCKLE That was hardly the way to be accepted by the 'best people', whoever they were. How much do clothes matter?

BEATON In the first place a great deal. In the long run not at all.

BUCKLE You didn't make much headway at Harrow or Cambridge?

BEATON Hardly any.

BUCKLE But on a flying visit to Oxford you thought you were really seeing life. Gathorne-Hardys, Eddie Sackville-West, David Cecil 'rattling on' . . . Puffin Asquith talking in 'spasmodic jerks' . . .

BEATON Oh yes!

BUCKLE You were always picking up hints – 'Never

relight your cigar'. And of course you noticed everything. Daddy pronouncing 'figure' 'feeguire', Lytton
Strachey's 'genteel dairy-maid voice', Fred Astaire in
Stop Flirting, making the word 'marvellous' sound
'clean and manly'.

BEATON After seeing him I wanted to cut my hair very
short.

BUCKLE Did you consciously model yourself on certain
actors? I'm trying to think of some who were supposed to behave like gentlemen on the stage – Gerald
du Maurier.

BEATON As a matter of fact, when I was quite young, in
Hampstead, *he* used rather to admire *me*. His
daughters were about my age. He was struck by some
expressions I used – yes, 'unfunny' was one.

BUCKLE Did you invent 'unfunny'?

BEATON I think I must have, Gerald du Maurier
copied me. He was very amused.

BUCKLE Through your photography you got to know
people.

BEATON Margot Oxford was very much in favour of
me from the start, and the Sitwells made it all seem
so easy and such fun. They helped me to get my first
exhibition at the Cooling Galleries.

BUCKLE Then there was Alannah Harper – wasn't she
what they called a 'Bright Young Thing'? – and lots
of Guinness girls, and when you spent a week-end with
Stephen Tennant at Wilsford you felt you were
getting in the swim.

BEATON There were setbacks and snubs.

BUCKLE Two steps forward, one step back?

BEATON Virginia Woolf refused to be photographed –
not that she was in what you call society. She wrote
a beastly reply. And one day, when I was walking
down Bond Street, thinking how impeccably dressed
I was, in a well-cut brown suit, a very distinguished

looking man – I don't know who he was – shouted at me 'People like you ought to be shot!' It rather sapped my self-confidence.

BUCKLE   As a photographer were you sometimes treated like dirt – shown in at the back door – that kind of thing?

BEATON   No. But Tony Snowdon was. At Wilton he was given his lunch with a bottle of beer in the pantry.

BUCKLE   Presumably *before* his marriage. One of your most gruesome setbacks must have been when those men ducked you in the river at the Wilton ball in 1927.

BEATON   I've never forgiven them. One of them became something high-up in the Army. I can't remember his name.

BUCKLE   Yet you went back into the Double Cube Room, dripping wet, and danced and behaved as if nothing had happened. Were many people bloody to you as an outsider?

BEATON   No, rather the opposite.

BUCKLE   Do you think your success in 'society' was due to your treating people as if you didn't give a damn?

BEATON   Not at all. I tried to be polite.

BUCKLE   Then you were the opposite of Beau Brummell. When Noël Coward ticked you off on the boat on your way back from your first trip to America, and told you your clothes were too exaggerated, your sleeves were too tight and your voice was too high, did you try to change?

BEATON   I couldn't, I wouldn't.

BUCKLE   Your first contract with Condé Nast in 1930, was that a big leg-up?

BEATON   Only from a money point of view.

BUCKLE   And when you published your first *Book of*

'People like you ought to be shot!'

Beauty in 1931 Lady Cunard threw it in the fire. 'He calls me a hostess, that shows he's a low fellow.'

BEATON   Then we became friends. I once saved her – there was a carrousel in a fair in Gerald Berners's park, and she was on one of the horses, and it went much too fast. She was terrified. I ran round and round, holding her on. I adored her.

BUCKLE   Suddenly, in the early 'thirties you seemed to know everyone in England, Paris, New York. Who do you think of as having exceptional distinction – in the way of behaviour, I mean?

BEATON   Gilbert Russell, Maud Russell's late husband. He was quite special, and he entertained an amazing mixture of people at Mottisfont. Then, I should say Mary Devonshire. Today, there is David Somerset.

BUCKLE   The next Duke of Beaufort?

BEATON   Yes. He can be very rude too.

BUCKLE   Somebody once told me 'You'll never get anywhere unless you are taken up by some powerful woman'. There are usually just one or two around. I suppose Anne Fleming took up Freddie Ashton and Lucian Freud.

BEATON   Well, it never happened to me, I'm afraid.

BUCKLE   Not Lady Colefax?

BEATON   Not really, though she invited me all the time. She wasn't powerful.

BUCKLE   Was Lady Hartwell?

BEATON   Pamela Berry? I suppose she got people jobs on the *Telegraph*.

BUCKLE   Wouldn't you say that it's a very attractive quality in a woman to make you feel you are the one person in the room she is absolutely enthralled by?

BEATON   Yes, it's rather an American thing. Mrs Vreeland has it – but she has everything, charm, wit, clothes and she does fantastic things with her make-up.

[8]

BUCKLE Do you think that tough nut Louise de Vilmorin had it?

BEATON Yes, a bit. I think Irene Worth is an exceptional woman. She has learnt everything and become so distinguished.

BUCKLE Of all the women you knew, who entertained best?

BEATON Lady Cholmondeley.

BUCKLE Philip Sassoon's sister?

BEATON Yes. She hardly tampered with the beauties of Houghton. I remember a tiny crammed pot of black iris – no flamboyant arrangements. Everything was perfect, food –

BUCKLE Better than with the Duchess of Windsor?

BEATON Oh, much. The Duchess brought in the American style of doing things.

BUCKLE You mean, frightfully good cocktails and so on?

BEATON Yes. But I thought a lot of her. I respected and admired her all along.

BUCKLE You were on kissing terms before her marriage. Might it have gone against you that you took the photographs at their wedding?

BEATON Perhaps. But it didn't. It was just after that – in the same year 1938 – that I was sent for to photograph the Queen, the present Queen Mother.

BUCKLE Zooming ahead through the post-war years (I'm looking at your Diaries), you're staying with Diana and Duff Cooper at the British Embassy in Paris, you're designing a lot for the stage, you're *not* marrying Greta Garbo – was that a setback?

BEATON For her, I should say. She'd have been much happier.

BUCKLE And the Queen Mother arranged for you to take the official Coronation photographs. At a ball at the American Embassy you had a jolly talk with the

[9]

Queen, who warned you that the crown came down to '*here*', and then you thanked the Queen Mother and she 'laughed knowingly with one finger high in the air'.

BEATON I always thought her irresistible.

BUCKLE I haven't talked about your friendship with artists – Gide, Picasso, Cocteau, Tchelitchev, Bérard, Francis Bacon. Here are a few pages covering six months from November 1960 to August 1961.

BEATON My God! What is coming?

BUCKLE A bit of everything. Just to give a sort of blurred action picture of your cosmopolitan whizzing – November, staying with Anna-Maria Cicogna in Tripoli; January in New York, designing *Turandot* and seeing Garbo, scoring off Larry Olivier; Truman Capote in London and first sight of Nureyev; June, Jackie Kennedy dining with the Jakie Astors, and as she's leaving you say to her 'When you bugger off, we're going to have a wonderful *post mortem*'; visit to Augustus John; Barbara Hutton's ball at Tangier in August; then Countess Volpi's ball in Venice –

BEATON Anna-Maria's Tripoli house was so lovely. An endless enfilade of white rooms, tropical plants and a curtain of water disappearing out of sight in the courtyard –

BUCKLE The point is you'd come a long way from the young man who was dying of frustration during summer holidays with his 'nice, ordinary middle-class family' at seaside places like Sheringham and Bournemouth. You must sometimes have felt you were really seeing life at last.

BEATON I don't think I did.

BUCKLE In that case, you were the exact opposite of Chips Channon. One always suspects that after a particularly brilliant dinner-party Chips went home and drew coronets in his diary.

BEATON   I know what you mean. But I was always too taken up with my work to think about society.

BUCKLE   Well, Society *was* your work in a sense. That's why you were so good at photographing it.

BEATON   As we get older work takes possession of us and leaves no room for either ambition or self-pity.

BUCKLE   So, having climbed the ladder and won the game and become the greatest social success of our century in two continents, you didn't feel any sense of achievement?

BEATON   None.

The Peerage and the Aristocracy

PATRICK MONTAGUE-SMITH
EDITOR DEBRETT'S PEERAGE

What is the definition of an aristocrat? As with the word 'commoner,' it means different things to different people. Some equate 'commoner' with one who was born non-Royal, even though he or she is as aristocratic as it is possible to be. A case in point is The Queen Mother, daughter of the fourteenth Earl of Strathmore and Kinghorne, head of an ancient house, with a forebear in a direct male line who married a daughter of the King of Scots.

Others understand the word to mean one who has no peerage or no title or style emanating from a peerage, such as the wife of the late Duke of Windsor and the present Duke of Gloucester. If we cross to the continent, the Queen of Sweden and the Princess of Monaco had no title before their marriages. (Whether a baronet's daughter is understood to be a commoner in this sense, such as the Duchess of Kent, is a moot point.)

More accurately, a commoner means one who is eligible to vote for a seat in the House of Commons. Thus Marquess Douro, son and heir of the Duke of Wellington, and theoretically, Prince Michael of Kent would qualify. But I have yet to meet anyone who would call them commoners.

So it is with the word aristocrat. Many would parallel the term with a peer and peeress, but surely it does not include all of them? There are those, particularly life peers, who restrict the use of their title to their presence

Some equate 'commoner' with one who was born non-Royal.

in the House of Lords, and continue to live as simply as they did before their elevation. Some would say that they accepted the honour merely to obey a Prime Minister who wanted them in the Upper House.

Even if we accept this definition for a peer and peeress, how far does it descend in a family? Children and those with courtesy styles perhaps, but what of the children of a younger son? If a peer has his grandchildren to stay, are only those of his eldest son aristocrats and the others merely commoners? This does not make sense.

An aristocrat can surely be a member of an untitled family. I was going to say 'of the landed gentry,' but what of those whose ancestors held extensive lands in Tudor times yet own no land but the garden of a house today? Perhaps not even that, for many lease a house or rent a flat. Yet this scion of an ancient house may be a near relation of a duke, going to the same school and belonging to the same clubs.

It would take a braver man than me to adjudicate on such matters, but I suppose the usually accepted opinion of an aristocrat is he who lives and behaves like one, just as in the seventeenth century a gentleman was often so described because he lived like one, even though he may have had a far richer neighbour who was called a yeoman, because of his coarser mode of life.

Although one cannot assess the nobility of a family according to the precedence officially assigned to him, few Englishmen would dispute that The Queen's senior subject after the Royal Family in all senses but one (for the antiquity of the Howards is surpassed by several families), is the Duke of Norfolk, Earl Marshal of England, Premier Duke and Premier Peer. Though the *Complete Peerage* and *Debrett* assign his present Dukedom from 1514 – that is from the creation of the 2nd Duke, the hero of Flodden Field, and not from his father who received the Dukedom in 1483 from Richard III – this is only of academic interest. He has precedence from 1397 and, as Earl Marshal has an official place above all Dukes. Not only that, but as the Duke ultimately derives the Norfolk title, through the Mowbrays, from Thomas of Brotherton, Earl of Norfolk, son of Edward I, in a sense he is a scion of the Royal Family. The Earldom of Arundel was inherited from the Fitz-Alans, of the same Breton stock as the Royal Stewarts or Stuarts.

There is undoubted glamour attaching to strawberry leaves as the highest and most exclusive grade of the peerage. At present there are 26 non-Royal Dukes (including Fife, created by Queen Victoria upon her grandson-in-law, but excluding the Duke of Edinburgh). Strangely enough, although the Duke of Edinburgh is a 'HRH' with precedence next to The Queen, he ranks as the most junior Duke in the House of Lords. It is most unlikely that there will ever be another Duke outside the Royal Family.

Excluding the quasi-royal Dukedom of Fife, the last non-Royal Dukedom was Westminster, created in 1874 by Queen Victoria. Although the Grosvenors were Cheshire baronets of ancient lineage, they acquired their wealth and extensive lands in Mayfair and Belgravia from the heiress Mary Davies, who in 1677 married the 3rd baronet. Her father, Alexander Davies, started life as a humble scrivener, but his great-uncle was the rich Hugh Audley, Lord of the Manor of Ebury. These lands were going to John Rea, but the two quarrelled over some missing deeds and jewels, and Audley revoked the settlement. Two other senior relations in turn were entailed these lands, but in the course of time Audley changed his mind in favour of young Davies.

It was rumoured that when that great commoner (here I am using the term correctly!) Sir Winston

Churchill retired as PM, that he was to be given for the first time the Dukedom of London, but he preferred to remain Sir Winston, KG, member for Woodford.

On looking at a hundred-year-old peerage it is remarkable to find that the list has changed so little. Only the Dukedoms of Leeds (1694) Buckingham and Chandos (1822) and Cleveland (1833) have died out, Leeds as recently as 1964. Amongst other peerages of the Duke of Buckingham was Lord Kinloss in the Peerage of Scotland, and this is possessed by his descendant the present Lady Kinloss. Cleveland is now represented by his kinsman, Lord Barnard. The *Complete Peerage* comments thus on the choice of a title:

It is a cause of wonder that the head of the historic house of Vane of Raby, himself the holder of a peerage of some antiquity (1699), should have so prided himself on a *bastard* descent from an infamous adulteress, that when he obtained a step in the Peerage, he changed his title to that of *'Cleveland'*, a peerage conferred on his notorious ancestress as the actual wages of her prostitution, and one which had stunk in the nostrils of the nation during the 40 years she enjoyed it; one too which had not been redeemed from the slur thus attached to it by any merit of her successors, of whom the one was a fool and the other a nonentity . . .

So much for Barbara Villiers, one of the mistresses of Charles II.

After the Duke of Norfolk was beheaded in 1572 for wishing to marry Mary Queen of Scots (the Dukedom was not restored until the Restoration), there were no Dukes outside the Royal Family until 1633. James I then bestowed the Dukedom of Buckingham on his favourite, George Villiers. 'Steenie' as James called him, had rapid promotion in the peerage. He was made a Baron and Viscount in August 1616, followed by that of Earl of Buckingham in the following January, and a year later, on New Year's Day 1617, as Marquess of Buckingham. As the Court was then getting restive,

[16]

King James thought he had better cut out the investing ceremony, which had always previously taken place when peers were created. According to the Harleian Manuscript 5176, folio 41B, the King, 'in his wisdom wished to avoid counterposition and competition of others.' Except for one or two later instances, these ceremonials were discontinued. Eventually the ceremony of taking a seat in the House of Lords was established in lieu.

The Buckingham titles terminated in 1687 when Steenie's son, the 2nd Duke, died of a chill caught while hunting in Yorkshire. According to Pope:

> *In the worst inn's worst room, with mat half hung*
> *The floor of plaster, and the walls of dung,*
> *On once a flock bed but repaired with straw*
> *With tape-tied curtains never meant to draw*
> *The George and Garter dangling from that bed,*
> *Where tawdry yellow strove with dirty red,*
> *George Villiers lies.*

The second English Dukedom after Norfolk is Somerset. As a romantic family the Seymours vie with the Howards. They each supplied a Queen for Henry VIII, and there were romances and marriages with Katherine, sister of Lady Jane Grey, and two generations later with Lady Arabella Stuart. Both these Royal ladies languished in the Tower, and both died in captivity. Like Norfolk, the Dukedom of Somerset was attainted – in this case when the 1st Duke and Protector was beheaded in the reign of his nephew, Edward VI – until the Restoration. It was then touch and go if the claimant would regain the honour from Charles II. He was aged 73 and near to death. The Marquess of Worcester was anxious to become Duke of Somerset himself, as had been his ancestor in the Wars of the Roses. He exhibited a promise by Charles II, but some of the documents were held to be forgeries. King

Charles restored the Dukedom to William Seymour, Marquess of Hertford, who died barely a month later; and Worcester in time received the Dukedom of Beaufort in lieu.

The Beauforts are of great interest for they are of Plantagenet stock from John of Gaunt by his mistress and later third wife, Katherine Swynford. Henry Beaufort, Duke of Somerset, had an illegitimate son known as Charles Somerset, who became Earl of Worcester. In time the descendants of the Beauforts, Dukes of Somerset became Somersets, Dukes of Beaufort.

Charles II was generous to his mistresses and bastard sons, some of both getting Dukedoms. Four creations to the sons have survived: Buccleuch, Richmond, Grafton and St Albans.

The Russells Dukes of Bedford probably owe their rise to power from being minor Dorset squires, to the prowess of John Russell in speaking fluent Spanish, perhaps acquired from the family connexion with the wine trade. In 1506 a ship from the Netherlands bound for Spain, carrying the Archduke Philip and his wife Joanna (sister of Katherine of Aragon), was wrecked off Weymouth. The principal landowner, Sir Thomas Trenchard, was alerted, who welcomed his Royal visitors to Wolfeton. There is a tradition that he sent word to his kinsman and neighbour, John Russell, to attend, since his visitors spoke no English and no one else knew Spanish. Russell is said to have accompanied them to Windsor, where he attracted the attention of Henry VII. Soon afterwards he became the King's gentleman usher, embarking on a career which led in 1550 to the Earldom of Bedford.

In 1694 William III raised the 5th Earl of Bedford to be Duke of Bedford. The marriage of his son to the heiress of the Wriothesleys brought the family the enormously valuable Bloomsbury estate. A later Duke said 'If one hadn't a few acres in London in these times of agricultural depression, I don't know what one would do.'

The Devonshires owe their greatness to that impressive character Bess of Hardwick, 'Building Bess,' who acquired the fortunes of all her four husbands, which she left almost entirely to her son, William Cavendish. In 1605 he became a Baron, and then, in 1618, Earl of Devonshire. William III made the 4th Earl, Duke of Devonshire, just one day junior to Bedford. Their princely wealth is proverbial, and the grandeur of Chatsworth has been envied by many a Royal scion.

As well as rewarding his English supporters, William III honoured the Dutch friends who accompanied him to England. His prime favourite and inseparable companion from youth was Hans William Bentinck, and at his coronation he created him Earl of Portland. Later the King transferred his affections to the good looking young Arnold-Joost Keppel, Baron van Keppel, who had been his page of honour and subsequently Groom of the Bedchamber. In 1697 Keppel was made Earl of Albemarle and received large tracts of forfeited Irish lands. The King's rift with Portland was only healed by a reconciliation on William's deathbed.

In 1716 George I made the 2nd Earl, Duke of Portland. The family acquired vast wealth when his son married the great heiress Lady Cavendish Harley, whom Prior called 'my noble lovely little Peggy.' She inherited the vast estates of the Cavendishes, including Welbeck Abbey. Her ancestors, the Dukes of Newcastle, also descended from Bess of Hardwick. The 3rd Duke of Portland, who married another Cavendish, daughter of the Duke of Devonshire, added the name of Cavendish before Bentinck. Incidentally, the Countess of Strathmore, mother of The Queen Mother, was a Cavendish-Bentinck.

[19]

An example *par excellence* of how a family built up
its power by marrying a succession of heiresses, is reflected by a swift advance up the peerage scale in the
Leveson-Gower family. The Gowers were Yorkshire
landowners, who acquired a Baronetcy from James I.
In 1668, the future 4th Baronet acquired large estates,
including Trentham, Staffordshire, from his mother's
family, the Levesons. As the result of further marriages to heiresses of the Granvilles (previously Gren-
villes), Earls of Bath, the Egertons, Dukes of Bridgewater, and finally to the greatest heiress of all, the
Countess of Sutherland in her own right, with over a
million acres in the north of Scotland, including most of
the counties of Sutherland and Caithness, they climbed
the ladder from being Baronets to Dukes in four suc-
cessive generations. The 5th Baronet in 1703 became
Lord Gower, his son in 1746 Earl Gower, his son in
1786 Marquess of Stafford, and finally his son in 1833
Duke of Sutherland.

Wraxall, in 1836, commented 'his vast property,
when added to his alliances of consanguinity or of marriages with the first ducal families in this country, the
Rutlands, Bedfords, Dorsets and Bridgewaters, ren-
dered him one of the most considerable subjects of the
kingdom.'

The choice of Sutherland as a name for his Dukedom,
said to have been suggested by Princess Augusta, can be
criticized, since the Dukedom is restricted to the male
line and able to part company from the ancient Scottish
Earldom of that name. This happened in 1963, when
the 5th Duke's niece became Countess of Sutherland in
her own right. The Dukedom reverted to the male heir,
the 5th Earl of Ellesmere. His line started with Lord
Francis, younger son of the 1st Duke, who took the
name of Egerton as the eventual heir of the Egertons,
Dukes of Bridgewater. On arrival in Lancashire, this

first Earl of Ellesmere found Worsley, the Bridgewater seat, 'a god forsaken place, full of drunken rude people, with deplorable morals.' But, with his improvements, he turned this into 'a civilized region.'

Two Dukedoms arose through the outstanding military services of John Churchill, Duke of Marlborough, and Arthur Wellesley, Duke of Wellington. Marlborough became successively in 1682 Lord Churchill of Eyemouth in the Peerage of Scotland, three years later, Lord Churchill of Sandridge, and in 1689, Earl of Marlborough. Then, in 1702, on the accession of Queen Anne, Duke of Marlborough. A splendid but concocted pedigree had been drawn up for his father, the cavalier Sir Winston Churchill, starting from 'an ancester' who came over with the Conqueror. An enemy of the family declared that, on the contrary, John Churchill's great-grandfather was a blacksmith who worked in the family of Meggs. There is a record that the Duke's great-great-great-grandfather Roger Churchill did marry the widow of Nicholas Meggs of Bradford Peverell. 'This,' said the Sir Winston of our day, seems very suspicious, and even disquieting.'

Arthur Wellesley, the Iron Duke, is unrivalled in our history for the number of honours and awards he received in his long lifetime, including all the five grades of the peerage. In 1809 he became Lord Douro and Viscount Wellington. Then early in 1809, Earl of Wellington, and later that year, Marquess of Wellington. Finally in 1815, he became Duke of Wellington. For the rest of his life he was just 'the Duke'. There is some continuity from Waterloo to World War II, when it is remembered that his godson and namesake, Prince Arthur, Duke of Connaught (third son of Queen Victoria), lived until 1942.

After Dukes come the Marquesses, of whom there are 38. The last, Willingdon, was created in 1936, and doubtless this really *will be* the last. (Dukedoms will probably be given to princes, with Earldoms for use by their heirs.) Though not vying with Dukes in popularity and antiquity, they seem a more prosaic lot. With a history which only goes back to the fourteenth century, the rank has not yet acquired a British ring (It is astonishing how many people ask if the wife of a Marquis is a Marquess). Though officially spelt Marquess, some prefer the French spelling, including Scotsmen in memory of the 'auld alliance.' All national newspapers follow suit, except *The Times*, to save one letter of newsprint.

The word means one who governs a march or borderland, but these duties had ceased before it was introduced to the Peerage. As the German equivalent was *Markgraf*, anglicized to Margrave, it was perhaps significant that Richard II, who introduced the title to England, was brother-in-law of the Margrave of Brandenburg. In 1385 he made his current favourite, Robert de Vere, Earl of Oxford, the Marquess of Dublin. The Earls strongly objected to losing their precedence by a new rank sandwiched between Dukes and themselves, with the result that the patent was cancelled. The favourite, instead, was given a Dukedom, the first outside the Royal Family.

The next recipient, John Beaufort, did not appreciate being a Marquess, which was recorded variously as Dorset and Somerset. He later begged the King not to restore this particular title, 'as the name of Marquess is a strange name in this kingdom.'

The premier English Marquessate, Winchester, was a Tudor creation. The first was Sir William Paulet, Lord High Treasurer to Edward VI, Mary I and Elizabeth I. It was he who, when asked how he managed to survive the changes, answered 'By being a willow, not an oak.'

Latterly, Viceroys of India, such as Reading, Linlithgow and Willingdon were rewarded with Marquessates. When relations of King George V in 1917 were asked to give up their German titles they were given Marquessates in lieu, namely Prince Louis of Battenberg received Milford Haven, his nephew Carisbrooke, Queen Mary's eldest brother the Duke of Teck became Marquess of Cambridge, but her younger brother Prince Alexander only received the Earldom of Athlone.

There are 200 or so Earls, representing by far the oldest grade of the peerage, with a history going back to the pre-Conquest Ealdormans, many of them representing historic houses in England, Scotland and Ireland. The three oldest in England, Shrewsbury (1442), Derby (1485) and Huntingdon (1529) are known as 'the Catskin Earls' reputedly because after these creations ermine was substituted for catskin on their robes. Several of these families have married into the Royal Family, such as Dalhousie, Strathmore, Harewood and Airlie; and an Earl is reputed to have said, 'My title is better than any of the dukes.'

In Scotland precedence goes by the Union Roll of 1707, when the Government there was united to England. The premier Scottish Earl is Crawford (1398), but this creation is long preceded by that of the Earldom of Mar, a rank translated from the ancient Mormaers of Mar, whose origin is 'lost in antiquity.'

Earldoms were the rewards given to Prime Ministers on leaving the Commons, such as Beaconsfield for Disraeli, Oxford and Asquith for Asquith and Avon for Sir Anthony Eden. In the same way retiring Speakers received Viscountcies.

Viscounts, the fourth rung in the peerage ladder, is also the most junior in date. Henry VI created the first Viscountcy in 1440 upon John, Lord Beaumont. As he was Count of Boulogne and Viscount of Beaumont in the sister kingdom of France, his new title enabled him to rank in England above mere Barons; and it was for the same reason that the next Viscount was also Count of Eu in Normandy.

The premier, and in fact only Viscount in the Peerage of England, is Hereford (1550). Lord Hereford's collateral ancestor, Elizabeth's Essex, was also 3rd Viscount Hereford. For some reason the title was popular in Ireland. Of the 24 which still survive, most date from the eighteenth century. In the Peerage of Scotland, Falkland (1620), which is a family unconnected with that country, and Arbuthnott (1641), were joined last year by the Viscount of Oxfuird (1651) after 272 years of dormancy. All the rest belong to the Peerages of Great Britain or the United Kingdom.*

There are naturally more Barons than those of the senior grades in the peerage. Included in this wide range of peers and peeresses in their own right are those whose predecessors fought in France, Scotland and Wales in the Middle Ages, and today Trade Union leaders, industrialists and others who have life peerages. The premier Barony is held by Baroness de Ros (1264). Others include such historic names as Lord Mowbray, Segrave and Stourton, Lord Clinton, Lord Zouche and Lord Saye and Sele. North of the border there are many with such stirring names as Lord Forbes, Lord Gray, Lord Elphinstone and Lord Lovat. The Irish Lord Inchiquin can trace his male line descent from Brian Boru, King of Ireland who was slain in 1014. On the strength of this he was once offered and declined the kingship of Ireland.

Many peerages have passed through the female line

* I here refer, of course, to those Viscounts who appear as such on the Roll of the House of Lords. There are others held by peers of senior grades. For instance, the Earl of Mar and Kellie is also Viscount Fentoun, the premier Viscount in the Peerage of Scotland.

several times over, since most of the oldest English Baronies were created by writs of summons to attend parliament. For most cases this was before patents of creation came on the scene, and it was held that these peerages passed to or through co-heirs, which were often subject to the particularly complicated and peculiarly English system of abeyances. Scotch titles sometimes passed to the female line, but fortunately the system of abeyance was never taken up.

There is no Welsh peerage, but some Welsh peers have lineages which rival the Irish in the length of pedigrees. Lord Mostyn shares with the Royal Tudors a descent from Marchudd ap Cynan, a 10th century chieftain, whose lineage ultimately goes back to Coel Hên who lived in the north before the departure of the Romans. Lord Milford, an old Etonian and our only communist peer, can trace back to Cadifor Fawr of Dyfed, a contemporary of William the Conquerer. His family claimed a much earlier origin, which takes some believing! Their pedigree reads: 'Cadifor was of the same tribe with Vortigern King of Britain, and paternally descended from Maximus, King of Britain and Emperor of Rome.' This is reminiscent of the Kaisers's boast that the Hohenzollerns were descended, through the Colonnas, from Julius Caesar.

For the most part, our noble families have thoroughly deserved their honours, but occasionally they were acquired in an unorthodox way, such as during Lloyd George's Administration, and by the activities of the honours tout, Maundy Gregory, which led him to gaol. Something similar occurred in the seventeenth century. In contra-distinction to the paucity of Elizabeth I's peerages and knighthoods, her successor James I was not only absurdly lavish with them, but he, and even more, his friend Buckingham, traded in honours for profits. In 1624 Sir Francis Leake paid £8,000 for his

Barony of Deincourt, and Lord Houghton gave £5,000 for an Earldom. In 1621 a Barony could be purchased for £10,000, when at least five were sold, and the same sum was asked to convert a Barony into an Earldom. A few years later the price dropped.

Many peerage families acquired their lands and wealth, and sometimes titles, through heiresses. It is laudable for them to adopt their names, but the fact that such descents are on the distaff side is often forgotten. Thus Baylys became Pagets, and ultimately Marquesses of Anglesey, the Adams became Ansons and Earls of Lichfield and the Roberts became Cokes, Earls of Leicester. The Shelleys, on inheriting Penshurst, became Sidneys, which is the surname of Viscount De L'Isle.

When Sir Hugh Smithson, a Yorkshire baronet, married the Percy heiress, he changed his name to Percy and took his seat as Earl of Northumberland. He then asked his king, George II, for the Garter, saying he was the first Earl of Northumberland not to be given this honour. The King replied he was the first Smithson to ask for it. Nevertheless, six years later, he was given the Order, and after a further ten years he became Duke of Northumberland.

When blood does not pass with lands, a change of name is less understandable. The present Earl of Lytton, by male descent, was originally Wiggett, later Bulwer, but he has no blood of the earlier Lyttons of Knebworth.

I, for one, regret that since the Crown, which is held under the hereditary principle, and now more popular than ever before, this same principle is held by many people to be wrong for lesser beings than the Sovereign, such as the legislators of the Upper House of Parliament.

In 1621 a Borony could be purchased for £10,000.

Language: U and Non-U
Double-U, E and Non-E

PROFESSOR ALAN S. C. ROSS, PHILIP HOWARD,
RICHARD BUCKLE IN A SYMPOSIUM

ROSS My essay, 'U and non-U', appeared in *Noblesse Oblige*, which was published in 1956.* But I really started the work for my U and non-U when I was an undergraduate at Balliol in the later 'twenties. In a previous article I coined the expressions 'U' and 'non-U'. They were to be applied to linguistic matters; 'U' means 'Upper Class' and 'non-U' means 'not Upper Class'. Thus I pointed out that to pronounce 'Derby' with the first syllable rhyming with 'cur' is non-U; in U speech the first syllable rhymes with 'car'. Or, again, that to say 'Pleased to meet you', on being introduced to someone is non-U.

It is natural to wonder whether matters have changed since *Noblesse Oblige* appeared in 1956 and this is, from what I have said above, almost equivalent to asking whether they have changed since 1926, that is, in the last fifty years.

The answer is that the antitheses between U and non-U have *not* changed. To pronounce 'forehead' almost as if it were two words is just as non-U to-day as it was in 1956 or 1926; the U make – and made – it

---

* This essay was essentially a non-learned version of an article 'Linguistic class-indicators in present-day English', which had appeared in 1954, in the Finnish learned journal, *Neuphilologische mitteilungen*.

rhyme with 'horrid', and that old favourite non-U 'serviette'/U 'napkin' is still in full force.

I have found one antithesis that has vanished. The U used to say 'wireless', the non-U 'radio'. Now nearly everyone says *radio*. And there is an antithesis new since 1956; the non-U say 'handbag' for the thing a woman carries; the U just say 'bag', ambiguous as this is.

BUCKLE I'm sure 'bag' was U and 'handbag' non-U as early as I can remember – even before *I* was an under-graduate at Balliol in the mid-'thirties!

HOWARD I can see that I am going to have to cast my-self as Thrasymachus in this symposium. You will re-member that he was the paper tiger at the beginning of the *Republic* who defined justice in simple Marxist terms as merely the interest of the ruling class, so providing Socrates with an intro and an Aunt Sally. I would not go so far as to define U as merely the vocabulary, idiom, pronunciation, and fetishes of people educated before the war at old-fashioned prep and public schools and bloody Balliol, but—

BUCKLE Balliol was, in fact, a rather non-U college. Brains, blacks, earnest Scotsmen, Rhodes Scholars. In my day the Master of Balliol was a socialist.

ROSS — who became a peer. I think the differences between the U/non-U picture of 1956-26 and that of today do not lie in the antitheses; these still survive. What the differences do consist of is a great accretion of new non-U words, expressions and clichés, coupled with a few non-U pronunciations.

HOWARD In my opinion the difference between 1956 and 1978 is far more fundamental than you state. Twenty-five years ago it was possible to draw distinc-tions between those who said 'lavatory' and those who said 'toilet', those who sat in the 'lounge' and those who lounged in the 'sitting-room', those who used 'napkins' and those who used 'serviettes', those who had 'dirty clothes' and those who had 'soiled linen', and those beasts who committed fish-knives, and were accordingly in a class of their own beyond the pale. Some of the distinctions may even have been true as well as witty and good fun. Even then, I suspect, the distinctions were not quite as clear as they were drawn. Language as a class-indicator was never black and white, but, like most things, muddy grey. Some U people always talked non-U. In any case, since those days, I have to tell you, Professor, that there has been a social revolution in language as in other things. We are all equal these days, or, at any rate, we are all nervously wearing masks ... Mass education until sixteen, television, and the revulsion against that most unfashionable of deadly sins, élitism, have changed the way we speak and the way we live. U public school boys try to be as like their non-U and working-class peers as possible, in appearance, dress, taste for music, and language. To stand out as a snob or merely different is the deadly social solecism. Twenty-five years ago public-school boys hastened to hoist their old school ties as soon as they left school, as a badge that they were U or at any rate adult, depending on the school. Today they would not be seen dead in them.

BUCKLE   I am sure that the whole wave of lower-class influence in speech, clothes and behaviour began with Pop Music in 1956, the year of Rock 'n Roll and Elvis, as well as of Nancy Mitford and Professor Ross. Professor, can we have some more fruits of your research?

ROSS   Here are some non-U words and expressions, old and new. May I give them to you in the form of a list? Shout if you disagree.
'Gift' for 'present'; 'Costly' for 'expensive'; 'Portion'

(of something to eat) for 'helping'; 'Sultry' (of the weather); 'perspire' for 'sweat'; 'I don't recollect' – or 'recall' for 'I don't remember'; 'postage stamp' for 'stamp'; 'to pain' for 'to hurt'; 'settee' for 'sofa'; 'ice-cream' for 'ice'; 'flu' for 'influenza' –

BUCKLE Gosh! I don't agree. Everyone says 'flu'.

ROSS Well, perhaps they do. *I* don't.

BUCKLE Do go on.

ROSS 'Well-connected' meaning 'of good family'; the expression 'titled people'; 'cliquey', or 'toffee-nosed' meaning 'snobbish'; 'classy' for 'smart'; 'Have you any family?' meaning 'a wife and/or children'; 'Baby isn't half creating' – meaning, making a noise'.

BUCKLE That's three horrors in one sentence.

ROSS 'Escort' for 'a man who takes a girl to a dance'; 'Town' meaning 'London'; 'a select neighbourhood'; 'the neighbours'; 'Oxford accent' meaning U accent; 'kids', 'kiddies', 'hubby', 'fella'.

BUCKLE 'Fella' may be working-class – it's better than the genteel 'felleugh' – but it's also old-fashioned U. 'A most amusin' fella' has an Edwardian or even Regency ring, like 'What a pooty gel!'.

ROSS Yes, 'fella' meaning 'a chap', but not 'fella' meaning 'male' – 'That chimpanzee's a fella'.

BUCKLE OK. Hasn't 'Hubby' vanished from the earth?

ROSS Oh no, 'My hubby' goes on full force, at least in the Midlands. To continue with my list –
'I came like I said', instead of 'as I said'. 'Are you quite better now?', for 'quite well now'. 'I haven't seen you in years', instead of 'for years'. 'Shall I pour?', meaning the tea; 'Eggs are very binding', meaning constipating; 'Is the steak to your liking?' 'Jacket potatoes' for 'Baked potatoes'. In reply to an offer of, say, mustard: 'No, I don't use it'. 'Champers' for 'champagne'. 'We've got gin, whisky, wine or whatever, you name it, we have it'. 'God bless!' 'Thanking

[31]

you'. 'You're welcome'. 'Onions do repeat so', meaning you taste them long after you have eaten them. 'Manners!' – to oneself, after belching. 'Charming!' used sarcastically; 'Where is the cloakroom?' or 'the smallest room', for 'lavatory'. Printed on the door of the lavatory 'This is it'. 'Has he been taken bad?', meaning ill, particularly with diarrhoea. 'Trouble with my Charles de Gaulle', meaning gall-bladder. 'Who's going to do the crocks?', meaning the washing-up. 'Muggins here, I suppose', meaning, 'I will'. 'What's for afters?', meaning 'what is the pudding course?'. 'I'm partial to ice cream', for 'I like ices'. 'Cigarettes coming up', meaning 'I'm just going to give them to you'. 'Have you seen my lighter *at all*?' 'Language!' when someone swears. 'Chummy here' – meaning 'the chap beside me' – 'fancies the au pair', meaning 'is attracted to the au pair girl'. 'She's expecting', meaning pregnant. 'She's dead stupid' for 'very stupid'. 'Have you brought your over-night bag?' 'Where have I left my vehicle?' meaning car. 'Is that your dirty great Rolls?' 'Just the car for yours truly'. 'A bit parky, isn't it?' meaning cold. 'The weather's something chronic', meaning bad. 'Could you back down a bit?', meaning reverse. 'Oh, very crafty!' meaning 'well done'. 'Bye-bye'. 'Give me a tinkle.' 'Hey, what d'you think you're doing, Mister?'. 'Sorry, Reverend'. 'He's a real big-head', meaning conceited. 'It's nearly half-two', meaning 'half-past two'. 'Do you want a cooked breakfast?' meaning bacon and eggs, etc. 'No, just cereal' –

HOWARD Good grief! You don't mean to tell me 'cereal' is non-U. Is it the activity of munching the stuff that is dead common, like Bingo? Or is it merely the name? One of the most U men I know, a wise, witty, and urbane former Clerk of the House of Commons, refers to his cereal as 'flakes', without the

preceding corn. Might we not make a useful distinction between words that are non-U because the activities they describe are surburban-genteel or vulgar: the vocabulary of ballroom dancing, tonic wine, bow ties, doilies, and non-U words for which there is a U alternative, for example, football, footy, fitba and soccer?

BUCKLE   What on earth is fitba?

HOWARD   Fitba is Glesgy pronunciation of football. It is often aped by non-Glaswegians as a demonstration that they are braw lads like the rest of us.

BUCKLE   My God, are you Scotch in spite of your name? The Professor obviously is. I'd better watch it. Is 'soccer' still the U word for football? You never hear it now.

HOWARD   I think a generation ago there was a hazy class distinction between soccer, which was a working-class and non-U game, and rugger, which was U and played at most smart schools and schools that aspired to be smart. There has been a revolution in sport as in other things. Football has become the national game, sanctified in its U-ness by the support of such arbiters of elegance as Freddy Ayer and the late Anthony Crosland.

ROSS   What do you say to the word 'brochure', which seems to belong in the same class as 'cereal'?

HOWARD   The thing rather than the word must be non-U, because package holidays and tourist hotels on the Costa Brava that serve chips with everything are considered non-U. There seems to be no U synonym for the word. Therefore, if you have to talk about brochures, which may happen to any of us on a bad day, you are going to have to use it. Or is the U word 'papers'?

BUCKLE   Of course not. What about 'prospectus'? I think 'brochure' is a bogus French word anyway.

ROSS   How do you say 'garage'?

BUCKLE   As in French. The middle-class pronounce it to rhyme with 'barrage'. Lower-class is 'garridge'.

ROSS   Oh, I think 'garáge' with the accent on the second syllable is very old-fashioned. Some words *are* certainly non-U because the things they mean are non-U, *e.g.* 'chalet' at a holiday camp, 'sandwich spread', *'individual* fruit pies', 'chiffon pie' –

BUCKLE   What *can* that be? I hate the expression 'a salad', meaning cold meat or fish surrounded by wilting vegetation. 'Bloater paste'! Has the word 'potted meat' gone out?

HOWARD   *Gorn* out!

ROSS   A very common non-U habit is to put 'old' before the name of a friend (Old Joe) or public character (Old Heath), or even an object ('I must get out the old cycle').

BUCKLE   'What is that marvellous drawing over the loo in my bathroom?' 'Oh, that's the old Michelangelo' ... Sorry.

ROSS   Then there is the question of non-U pronunciations. Here are a few I have noted. 'Clique' to rhyme with 'sick'. 'Café' to rhyme with 'gaff'. 'Buffet' to rhyme with 'stuffy'. 'Spinach' as 'spinnitch' instead of the U 'spinnidge' –

BUCKLE   Like Harwich or Norwich.

ROSS   'Madame Tussauds' as 'Madam Two-swords'. 'Marylebone' pronounced in full. 'Fiancé to rhyme with 'pie-fancy' –

BUCKLE   You are not quite precise. I've never heard anyone say 'Mary Lee Bone', but taxi-drivers often say 'Mar' (as in Kellie) 'Lebone'. The right pronunciation is, of course, 'Marry l' b'n'. And I should have thought the usual non-U way of saying 'fiancé' was 'feonn-say'. U people wouldn't use the word anyway.

ROSS   How about 'Riviera' pronounced as 'revere'er'?

[35]

BUCKLE   I think everyone says that, high and low. To have half a go at an Italian word and give up – that is, to say 'Rivvyairer' is surely a feeble compromise like 'ballay' for 'ballet'. To go the whole hog in Italian – 'Ree-vee-ay-rah' – would sound pedantic.

ROSS   Then there is the non-U tendency to accent the middle syllable in 'amicable', 'lamentable', 'coronary', 'preferable', 'marital' –

HOWARD   Surely that new accent on the second syllable is more *interesting* than merely non-U? Is it not an example of progressive accent, the reverse of the process that Fowler called recessive accent? There is a tendency for the stress to drift forwards as well as backwards, because we dislike a rapid succession of light syllables, and find them hard to pronounce.

Look at what is happening to 'formidable' and 'controversy', both often now accented on their second syllables, to the great indignation of those who became indignant about such matters. Perhaps these are non-U too? But then 'commendable' suffered the same fate some time ago, It used to be accented on its first syllable: "Tis sweet and commendable in thy nature, Hamlet.' Progressive accent shifted the stress forward one syllable in the nineteenth century, and all the dictionaries now recognize this as the correct, if not the U pronunciation. Anyway *de pronuntiationibus non disputandum*. Pronunciation changes even faster than vocabulary and idiom. We are tempted to think that the pronunciations of our childhood are frozen right for all time. Queen Elizabeth I and Queen Victoria would both sound distinctly non-U today.

BUCKLE   No doubt Queen Elizabeth I would sound to us like a farmer's wife; and Queen Victoria always thought herself dowdy in comparison with the haughty Whigs: but I am still 'one of those who become indignant' over such pronunciations, which we hear nightly on radio and television. You may be right that I am 'frozen' in the customs of my childhood but I do think – or rather, feel – that to pronounce 'exquisite' or 'lamentable', and particularly 'marital', with the accent on the middle syllable is vile. It is aesthetically offensive. I know the laws of beauty change, like everything else, but I should fight against that to the end of my days. Incidentally, can you imagine the French or Italians changing the pronunciation of a word like *'formidable'* or *'amabile'*?

ROSS   The non-U are extremely fond of clichés, many of them of a slangy nature. Here are some. 'Watch it!', 'Suit yourself', 'You heard', 'Fair enough', 'D'you mind?', 'Relax!', 'Let's face it', 'I give up', 'A bit dodgy', 'That's right' for 'yes', 'It's as simple as that', 'What seems to be the matter?', 'See what I mean?' (used as a punctuator, *i.e.* redundantly), 'I leant over backwards' (to understand a point of view), 'Don't do yourself an injury' (i.e. rupture yourself), 'When it comes to the crunch', 'I didn't quite catch' for 'I didn't hear you', 'I couldn't agree more', 'He got the message', i.e. understood, 'Can we have some service?' (in a pub), 'Leave it with me' for 'Leave it to me', 'I laughed like a drain', 'A touch of the Alf Smiths', meaning 'characteristic of Alf Smith', 'Linguistics – who needs it?', 'It's curtains for the old firm', 'The new job, it's a challenge', 'Believe you me', 'Like the man said', 'Are you with me?', 'He took three wickets on the trot', meaning one after the other, 'Don't tangle with him', 'Something like that' (meaning 'yes', in answer to a question), 'It's all part of the service' (responding to thanks), 'It's what we're here for' (likewise), 'How right you are', 'It's just one of those things', 'I'll spell it out', 'That shook me', 'We'll have to play it by ear', 'He's such a fool it just isn't true', 'I haven't a clue', 'Get off my back', 'Not to worry', 'Long time no see', 'Be my guest' for 'Help yourself', *e.g.*, to the telephone, 'Come again' meaning 'What?', 'Big deal', meaning the opposite, 'I'll go along with that', 'I threw the book at him', 'Please yourself' in reply to a demand for advice, 'You must be joking', 'What seems to be the trouble?' 'You're telling me', 'Just the job', What's he on about?', 'D'you mind?' 'Drop dead!', 'Goodbye now', 'Fancy that', 'Get lost', 'I saw him Monday, no, I tell a lie, it was Tuesday', 'George scored the first goal, all right?' 'I wouldn't know' for 'I don't know', 'How silly can you get?', 'That's your lot', meaning 'That's all that's due to you', 'So he fell off his cycle. I had to laugh', 'Was my face red?' meaning 'I was ashamed', 'I can't compete', 'This I must see' for 'I must see this', 'Bang on' for 'exactly right', 'That's the idea' for 'Yes', 'Back to square one', 'I follow' for 'I understand', 'Don't do anything I wouldn't do' (on saying good-bye), 'I couldn't care less'.

BUCKLE   I have several points. You have given us at least one Jewish form of speech. Some of the unattractive clichés you quote I believe to be in use among the U. I don't think you can dismiss all Americanisms as non-U. You seem to lump together middle-class and working-class expression.

ROSS   I never did distinguish between the genteel and the lower-class. Everything that was not U, I called non-U. I have some examples here, though, obviously originating in dialect, or even with the criminal classes, which have been popularised by television and which are all non-U. 'Lolly' for money, 'skint' for broke, i.e., without money, 'brass', also money, 'cuppa' meaning 'a cup of tea', 'to whip' or 'to nick' meaning 'to steal', 'git' as a term of abuse like 'bastard', 'butty' a kind of sandwich, 'chuffed' meaning 'pleased with oneself', 'I'll thump you', meaning 'I'll hit you', 'I'll do you', meaning 'I'll beat you up', or even 'I'll kill you', 'I've been conned', meaning 'cheated'.

BUCKLE These last examples only confirm me in my belief that the time has come when you *must* distinguish between middle-class genteelisms and working-class expressions. Nobody holds it against a West Country labourer when he says 'Oi be roight pleased about thaat'; whereas to use genteelisms like 'toilet' for 'lavatory' or 'passing on' for 'dying' is to aspire unsuccessfully to a more refined status; and to use clichés is a mindless, lazy and mistaken way of trying to be in the swim. Apart from 'brass' which is North Country, and 'butty', which I think is miners' slang, all the examples you give of low, even criminal, speech, Cockney in origin, are now absolutely U.

ROSS I must say I find that very hard to believe.

BUCKLE They are not even used in inverted commas. Any belted earl under fifty, and many over, will talk quite naturally about being skint when he is short of lolly, of having a kip and of being conned. 'Chuffed' is rarer, though I think anyone who served in the last war would have picked it up from his fellow soldiers. And you might add to this new lingo, which the upper class and the working class have in common, and which I would call Double-U, the words 'scoff' for 'food' or, as a verb, for 'to eat', 'pong' for a bad smell, and 'flog' for 'sell' – 'I've just flogged my Canalettos at Sotheby's'.

ROSS Are you really right about the earl? At all events he would use inverted commas.

BUCKLE I'm glad you brought that up, because, mistrusting my own judgment as I hardly ever go out,

'I've just flogged my Canalettos at Sotheby's'

I rang up a neighbouring earl who is (a) 39 (b) rather go-ahead in that he makes films and is always surrounded by dazzling young people (c) entirely respectable – in fact, Henry Pembroke – just to check. He said he used *all* those words *without* inverted commas.

ROSS   Oh.

BUCKLE   But he added that he wouldn't write them.

ROSS   I dare say a Cockney wouldn't *write* them, either.

BUCKLE   That is just what I said. Well, are you convinced? When you and Nancy Mitford published *Noblesse Oblige* I suppose a lot of socially aspiring people tried hard never to use the words 'mirror' or 'note-paper' again. I certainly noticed that some well-brought-up people who had only been half-conscious of saying 'looking-glass' or 'writing-paper' automatically, all their lives, made an effort to be common and to say 'mirror' and 'note-paper'; and they laughed at themselves self-consciously when they said 'a glass of sherry' instead of the vulgar 'a sherry'. Also in 1956 came John Osborne's play *Look Back in Anger* and the New Wave. From that moment the lower classes became the heroes and heroines of drama, instead of the comic relief, and the small-part secondary grotesque characters were taken from the upper-middle class. The black, downtrodden North Country came into its own, and only Yorkshire, Lancashire or Durham playwrights and novelists were acceptable. At the same time Pop Music was flooding the world and television was taking over. By 1964, the year of the Beatles' triumphant trip to America, boys were being sent home from school because their hair was too long, but within another two years the headmasters had given in. Then came marijuana, a great abolisher of class-distinction. Now, in 1978 U-people are using Cockney slang just as Christopher Sykes

[41]

foretold they would in *Noblesse Oblige*, and Professor Ross hasn't even noticed it.

ROSS Well, it's still only a very small part of the vocabulary.

HOWARD I think Richard Buckle's analysis is a perceptive and persuasive one. Snobbery has got a bad name these days, though it is still an infinite source of jest for and about the English. We are all equal now. Or at any rate, we are all careful to wear the mask. In that way it seems to me a more civilized society.

BUCKLE If I may return to the Professor's list and make a few specific comments. Just as 'brass' and 'He'll likely be here tomorrow' (for 'probably') are local expressions and, as such, to be encouraged, so the inversion in 'This I must see' is Jewish, and like other more self-consciously comic Yiddishisms – 'Now she tells me' – comes to us from Central Europe *via* Broadway. The whole question of American influence is vast. As I said before, you *can't* dismiss all Americanism as non-U.' Goodbye now', is rather non-U *in America*, like 'Take care!' (but not as bad as 'freshen up') – it sits oddly beside the Victorian-genteel 'Fancy that!' on your list. The greatest American influence comes from the world of gangster movies, and sometimes reaches us *via* Cockney. It is invariably terse, vivid and funny. 'Drop dead!' – to be heard at the most exclusive dinner-parties – is a good example. 'Get lost', 'Big deal!' and 'You must be joking' are others. 'Like the man said', meaning 'Do as you're told', is splendid, I think. On the other hand 'To play it by ear' and 'I'll go along with that' are surely Madison Avenue, like 'kicking around' an idea and much else. Genuine Cockney expressions are 'What's he on about?', 'I tell a lie', 'All right?' said threateningly, and 'Watch it!', also a threat.

ROSS The question of Americanisms is different.

When I first wrote I said 'OK' was the only U one, but as you say, I dare say there are others now.

HOWARD   Most of us are bower birds of language. We pick up the brightest new slang, Broadway, Yiddish, Cockney, and from other fertile sources of new language, to decorate our discourse with for a while. It becomes tarnished from overuse, and we drop it and pick up something else. Vivid new slang is a source of strength for the language. America, the great linguistic melting-pot, inevitably produces scum as well as shining new metals. Anyway, the young, both U and non-U, ape the language and appearance of the 'personalities' of the moment. A 'personality' being somebody who appears frequently on television, but has no other obvious talents. But, as I said before –

BUCKLE   *Like* you said!

HOWARD   *Like* I said, the real distinction today is between educated and uneducated speech – 'E' and 'non-E'.

ROSS   Of course, the U are in general not more educated than the non-U today. But in matters of speech they really seem to be so, and there are many non-U words and expressions which are, essentially, uneducated. For instance, '*very* unique'. 'Can I have a *lend* of your pencil?'; 'disinterested' meaning 'uninterested'; 'I better come' (instead of *I'd*); 'I would *of* come'; 'It is feasible that he will come tomorrow', *i.e.*, 'possible'; 'He was stood there on the court'; 'He's good at figures', *i.e.*, arithmetic; 'strata' used as a singular; 'infer' meaning 'imply', 'a classical situation', for 'classic'.

HOWARD   'Disinterested' is indeed commonly used as if it were an elegant synonym of uninterested. This is spoiling a useful word for all of us. It is vexing. It is non-E. It is illiterate. It is wanton waste. But is it also specifically non-U?

ROSS   Ah, no, it's more uneducated than non-U.

HOWARD   Your 'strata' used as a singular is a piece of sociologists' jargon. In the same way 'data' is becoming a singular in Computerese. They could be called non-E, or illiterate, if you take the stern view that Latin words must remain eternally unchanged when they pass into English. But consider what happened to 'agenda' and 'stamina', both similar Latin plurals, both now become English singulars. I have not noticed that this process is particularly non-U. It seems more like academic jargon. 'It is a notable *phenomena* that one *criteria* of education in an influential *strata* of society is to criticize what the *media* is saying about all this *data* on linguistic class-indicators.'

BUCKLE   The Professor will faint. Even I wouldn't use any of those words as a singular noun.

HOWARD   But words do change their number. According to his granddaughter, the great James Murray* used to say things like: 'These porridge are too runny.' Scots purists still treat porridge as a plural. What with cereal being non-U and porridge being plural, breakfast is a pretty unnerving meal these days. But language, if it is living, does change. English has survived immense changes. Think how worried thoughtful Anglo-Saxons must have been when they realized that the progressive simplification of their grammar, particularly the loss of gender in nouns, was leading them into linguistic isolation from the rest of Europe.

BUCKLE   What happened? Did they arrive from Europe in 600 AD with genders, and find four hundred years later that they had lost them?

ROSS   Yes. They had the three genders in Anglo-Saxon, and these got blurred just before the Norman Con-

* First editor of *The Oxford English Dictionary*.

[44]

quest. But gender remained in Kent until the 14th century.

HOWARD   Living languages are in a continuous state of change. Only dead languages stay still, which is why Latin and Ancient Greek are the best languages for grammarians. They can legislate for dead languages, without finding that the languages have moved on while they were writing, and made their rules about correctness and incorrectness obsolete. Language changes faster at some times than at others. The Age of Settlement was a period of great linguistic change, evolving Old English from the tribal dialects. Then, just as Middle English evolved in the period after the Norman Conquest, so Modern English grew from the Middle English dialect of London in another revolution, partly caused by the invention of printing. We may be at the beginning of one more linguistic revolution today, caused by the spread of literacy, television, radio, and the immense numbers of people at the round earth's imagined corners who are speaking and writing English. Their dialects flow into the central ocean of English, widening, enriching, and changing it.

BUCKLE   We musn't get started on the difference between French and English Literature – Racine with his few words *versus* Shakespeare with his many – but it's amazing, when you come to think of it, that you should speak approvingly of the widening, the enrichment and the changing of English, while the whole purpose of the Académie Française and their weekly meetings is to limit, to purify and to purge the French Language.

HOWARD   It is strange: but while the French have their Academy, we have Professor Ross.

BUCKLE   Whose motto is: Divide and rule.

HOWARD   Which brings me to jargon and clichés – two

'parameters of marketing interface'

French words, incidentally. Most of us are addicted to clichés. Language would *come to a grinding halt*, you could say, without them. Not all of us can blaze trails. We cannot each be Shakespeare, that superb recoiner of old clichés. Some clichés are in fact the simplest way of saying something: 'white elephant', 'Hobson's choice', 'a forlorn hope', 'riding one's hobby-horse'. You impoverish the language by depriving us of the useful ones. The otiose and silly clichés eventually become laughing-stocks and die of shame: 'leave no stone unturned' and 'no avenue explored', 'suffer a sea change', and so on. 'No way', and 'Right on', those vogue clichés of five years ago, are now as dated as Teddy Boys.

'Jargon' comes from a delightful old French word which means 'the twittering birds'.

BUCKLE   *Il n'y a bête ni oiseau*
         Qu'en son jargon ne chante ou crie . . .

HOWARD Well done. By the 15th century *'le jargon'* had come to mean the *'argot des malfaisants'*. In English it now has three principal meanings. First it can mean a medley of more than one language: this meaning is otiose. Second, it means the technical vocabulary of a science, trade, or other hermetic group. This sort of jargon is none of our business. If diplomats find it a useful esoteric shorthand in their mystery to talk of *'tours d'horizon'* and *'démarches'*, if journalists find it saves time to talk about 'a MUST', and businessmen 'parameters of marketing interface', that is their affair. If their jargon does not serve a useful purpose, it will soon die. The third kind of jargon in English is the nastiest. This is pretentious language conspicuous for its abstractitis, circumlocution and avoidance of plain English. Sir Winston Churchill said that Ramsay MacDonald could squeeze less thought into more words than anyone else he knew. Most of us are liable to fall into this kind of jargon occasionally, if we are not careful. It takes time to say things simply. This sort of jargon is a form of linguistic pollution. It is non-E. It is inefficient because it makes your meaning hard to understand. It flourishes in all classes and conditions of men, but most in universities, Whitehall, Westminster, Fleet Street and other spawning-grounds that are not obviously non-U. 'At this moment of time', 'Hopefully' meaning 'I hope', and all the other current bits of obfuscatory jargon seem to me endemic, not confined to one class.

ROSS   Well, hopefully is an American word, it's a translation of German *hoffentlich*, probably came in from Yiddish, which, after all, is in the main German.

HOWARD   Might I draw your attention to 'cheers' meaning thank you as a possible example of non-U. Do any small favour for a young Englishman these days and he will thank you by saying 'cheers'. The word has clearly escaped from the pub, where it was a popular drinking toast. Women tend to say 'lovely' for 'thank you' when you pay for something in a shop. Then, 'Sorry?' is coming to mean 'I beg your pardon, I did not hear that.' But when you bump into somebody, you say 'Cheers' rather than 'Sorry'. It is a sobering thought that this boozy word 'cheers' has become our most popular word for thanking and apologizing.

BUCKLE   While duly sobered, let us grind to a halt. Professor, your 'touch of the Alf Smiths' reminds me that I have long thought the phrase used by Chorus in *Henry V*, on the eve of Agincourt, to evoke the mateyness of our warrior king with his troops, was unattractively sentimental and non-U: 'a little touch of Harry in the night'.

ROSS   Cheers.

[48]

'a little touch of Harry in the night'

Clothes: The Well-Dressed Man

CHRISTOPHER SYKES

The Original 'Enquiry', carelessly entitled *Noblesse Oblige* and carelessly edited (if at all) by Nancy Mitford, came out as long ago as 1956. The little miscellany contained only one masterpiece, namely John Betjeman's poem 'How to Get On in Society', yet the book has gone on selling from the date of publication to the present. The subject is obviously one with much appeal.

I think there is a very obvious reason for this. In contradiction to and defiance of what legislators pretend to believe, and try to force us to pretend to believe too, human beings are very different. To some extent they can be classified. It's a shame that this should be so in an age which hopes to abolish classes, but such is the fearful and daunting fact. The best we can do is to smooth down class-differences so that they cause no unnecessary pain, so that we render them unobnoxious; but we are fools if we believe that we are able to abolish them. We do better if we manfully face the fact that class-distinctions are here to stay, because too much interest and history attaches to them, because human beings are made in such a way that they are inevitable.

The Abolitionist Movement may be hopeless, but it is strong nonetheless. As though to prove it, I have unwittingly offended against it thus early in these notes. I have used the word 'manfully' as a word of praise, and I am assured by the Reformers that of all class-distinctions, that which distinguishes the male from the female sex is the most horrid and disgusting. Laws have been passed to ensure that sex-distinctions are never noticed, and efforts to enforce them have been made with laughable results. I plead that I had no alternative to my use of the term 'manfully'. If I had said 'womanfully' I would have suggested the opposite of what I meant.

I shall defy the law. I shall go on the assumption that there are two classes, to one of which we all belong: one class we call Men, and the other class Women. Of course these two classes, like all other classes, overlap. There are effeminate men and masculine women, but neither of these are really *outside* their class. It is rarely a matter of serious puzzlement as to which class an effeminate man or a masculine woman belongs.

Writing in *Noblesse Oblige* in 1955 I attempted a picture of London manners and speech 100 years on, in 2055. Re-reading the fantasy in 1978, I see that I saw things going in a more orthodox Socialist fashion than in fact they have done, and in a more proletarian fashion. I overestimated certain prevalent tendencies and, like all foretellers of the future, including some very famous ones such as George Orwell and Aldous Huxley, I made little allowance for the power of reaction.

However, my aim was modest; I did not seek to change the path of history, so I am not unduly ashamed. Returning to the question of class distinctions at the present time, I have been asked by Dicky Buckle, the present editor, to confine my remarks to elucidating how these distinctions are expressed in our clothes. I did but touch on the subject once, and indirectly, in my previous article. I drew attention to the curious fact that while in U-Society umbrellas are used as a normal part of a well-dressed man or woman's equipment in the town, in the same society in the country, the use of umbrellas is strictly confined to women, a sole and rather puzzling exception being made in favour of clergymen.

[51]

Let me take up the subject at that point. My knowledge of umbrella custom has increased in the last twenty-two years. Soon after the book's appearance I had a meeting with Nancy Mitford at which we discussed this problem of holy men and umbrellas. Nancy soon lighted on the answer. It was a matter of town-clothes. There was nothing against an unordained duke or other profane male U-personage carrying an umbrella in the country at a race-meeting, or at the Agricultural Show, or at the local fête. Why? Because, at such festivals, town-clothes were worn, so umbrellas were allowed, and if the clergy seemed particularly prone to umbrellas, that was because they *always* wore town-clothes.

In 1955 I had never been to America. In 1959 I visited New York for the first time. I was overwhelmed by many startling and unforgettable impressions, but by none more powerfully than those conveyed by the local umbrellas. The summer weather was just breaking so one saw a lot of them. The United States was then the only Western country in the world where umbrellas were unisexual.

It is true that I do not remember seeing a female American using a large masculine Brigg-style umbrella, but I very often saw, in fact more often than not, men of obviously well-to-do environment, upper-crust types without question, using or carrying dainty little feminine umbrellas. Much observation led me to the conclusion that in the United States umbrellas are not regarded as objects in any way related to sex. They are looked upon by Americans simply as machines to keep off the rain, and their size and ornamentation, in so far as it has no utilitarian purpose, is considered quite irrelevant. The argument sounds sensible.

It sounded so sensible that it spread to European countries. By the 1960s unisexual umbrellas were commonplace in Germany. Men took to owning short stumpy ones which when folded could fit neatly into a despatch case or portfolio, and could also be used by women. Later this kind of umbrella-usage spread to France, also under the influence of the increasing numbers of American tourists, but with a difference: whereas in France the new usage was and is restricted to the young, in Germany men of any age can be seen carrying short unisexual umbrellas. As regards the class aspect of the innovation, there seems to be none in Germany, which defeat in World War II really did shake to the foundations; and while in France the elderly *gratin*-members are more conservative than anywhere in Europe so that they dress and use umbrellas, etc., with avoidance of any sort of innovation, the young react against this tendency and yield with apparent joy to such Americanisms as unisexual umbrellas and bad food. I am told that among Spaniards of all ranks umbrellas are confined to female usage, since for a man even to have one is regarded as an open sign of cowardice.

It is a fact, easy to forget today, that throughout history, from the earliest recorded time until quite recently, the fashion of clothes has been set by men and the same fashion reflected in female apparel. Many young women now wear jeans, trousers made of denim, cut very tight about the posterior. This is a fashion first designed for male wear, and not disagreeable when worn by a young man, provided he is not fat, but very unbecoming to female anatomy which it renders ugly and absurd. But the young women love their jeans, not least the feminists among them, unconscious that by wearing them they proclaim male dominance.

To consider a world of activity distant from the usual one of the jeans-wearers: the world of horsemanship. The traditional roles of male and female fashion

even to have one is regarded as an open sign of cowardice

lingered on here till recent times, in the hunting field especially, and are not quite extinct even now. They are to be seen where the men still, like the legendary Frenchman, dress for the horse, and the women ride sidesaddle. This is most often visible at horse-shows, especially in the 'dressage' classes. But the sidesaddle is unhappily slowly disappearing, and with it the riding habit. Almost all women ride astride today. Has this spurred women to invent wonderful riding clothes perhaps designed by the great fashion houses of Paris, Rome, and London? Not at all. It has spurred them to dress up as men, to appear in the showring in a cut-away coat and all the paraphernalia of 'the well dressed fox-hunting man' and canter away with the first prize for dressage, indistinguishable at a distance from a horseman. (I have known two men who, owing to war-wounds, had to ride side-saddle. Neither wore a habit.)

But if we consider a world in which the fact of two sexes is shamelessly acknowledged, a world not necessarily abnormally poor or abnormally rich but not excluding either, the utterly normal world to outside appearances, in which men wear trousers and women skirts, then we can only be amazed at the absolute absence of relation of male to female dress. They are conjoined only by coincidence, otherwise their different styles might be hundreds of years apart in time.

In 1945, with the end of World War II, there was much talk of a clothes-reform for men. It came to nothing. Most men who had been in the services rushed gladly to shed their uniforms (unless they had enjoyed spectacular promotion in which case they shed tears as well) and put on their peace-time suits in a victorious spirit. It was a time of mothballs for that was the prevalent smell of those years. It was also a time of nostalgia and one's suit seemed something for which one had fought. But there was no clothes-reform for a while. By the 'fifties there was a generation who had no first-hand experience of the war, only dim childish memories of life before 1939 and anxious, as all young people should be, to be free of the burden of the past; in short there was a younger generation. Then gradually there came clothes-reform of a sort.

It was a time of increasing socialism and increasing belief in egalitarianism. The latter was, to some extent, a hangover from the war and service life. No matter what Leftist propagandists say, class distinctions of the ordinary kind play very little part in service life, if only because the services have such strong class distinctions of their own. (If a ducal subaltern cheeks his lowly-born CO he is 'for it'.) A great many U-conventions had grown extinct through senescence. Up to 1939 it was a gaffe to wear a grey top-hat before Ascot or after Goodwood. After 1945 you could wear it all the year round, even in the snow, without being open to criticism. (In fact at the moment black silk top-hats show signs of obsolescence at Royal Garden Parties and weddings.) But the time was ripe for change, and the clothes-reform of the 1950s and 1960s took pride in its radicalism and was not concerned with the U-conventions of the past. Its aim was to invent new ones. For the first time in history since the French Revolution, it sought to evolve fashions from the apparel and habits of non-U classes. The chic men or women in France, England and the USA sought to be as proletarian as possible.

A striking feature of the young reformers was their dirt, and a striking feature of the dirt was less their unwashed hands, faces and clothes than their long straggling unwashed hair. An important and possibly enduring result of the reform following the Second World War was that it brought to an end the U-convention (originally French) and which had spread to the whole of Society that a decent male wore very short hair. Such a hairstyle was for long thought to indicate a necessary measure of virility. This belief showed ignorance of history for the custom seems only to have started in France in the 1860s, and to have been generally adopted in the 1880s to be killed in the ten years following 1960.

When the demobilized non-U mass turned to clothes-reform they did not take proletarianism for their model. They turned to nostalgia and, like most nostalgics, they longed for a past which had never existed, for an imagined Edwardian world of the early twentieth century, The movement was short-lived for two reasons. It depended too much on an element of fancy dress and it came to attract the attention of the criminal underworld. Robber and vandalistic bands called themselves the Teddy Boys and brought the law-abiding majority of Teddy Boys into disrepute. In one respect they were influential on their successors who dressed as Italians and wore pointed shoes. But such shoes, to be elegant, require to be made with great shoemaking skill, and the mass-produced variety, popularly known as 'winkle-pickers', were very ugly and came to pieces quickly. The movement passed and never reached the class it half-consciously parodied. There were no U-Teddy Boys.

But the U-proletarians went on, going from fantasy to fantasy, though mercifully they abandoned dirt and thus caused prosperity in the shampooing and setting industry. At one point they took to rags, wearing, that is to say, nothing so unimaginative as the genuine rags of poverty, but carefully and presumably expensively contrived rags of silk, fur and velvet, all artfully ripped, rent, slashed, patched and safety-pinned. Further fantasy was added to this mode of apparel by the wearing of chains, beads and other forms of collar and necklace. They went on with these novelties longer

prosperity in the shampooing and setting industry

than the genuine proletarian Teddy Boys and Italian-ates, but they were doomed for the same reason. There was too much element of fancy dress to make for per-manence, yet male clothing, static for more than the length of three lifetimes, was now a scene of turbulent revolution. There remained, however, one unchanged corner to which the non-U classes had drawn attention. This was the matter of shoes.

Shoes had shown themselves slow-coaches before. During more or less the whole of the eighteenth century shoes had remained virtually unchanged. It seems from pictures that it was only the size of the buckle that was liable to radical alteration and when about the end of the century buckles were abandoned, then the modern lace-up shoe gradually came into being.

The failure of 'winkle-pickers' led first to the 'cuban' heels popularized by the Beatles, then to a diametrically opposite preference for blunt square-tipped shoes, also with high heels. (It is forgotten that high heels for men began as part of a man's riding equipment and are worn, with an unavoidable mincing gait off the horse, by cow-boys to this day.) Next came platform-soles, which removed even the toes of the wearer an unprece-dented four inches from the ground. Among startling innovations is to be noted a revival in the early 1960s of elastic-sided boots, the traditional footwear of Dora, the mythological figure of the 1920s representing kill-joy Puritanism; oddly contrived pumps; cork-soled shoes; and, very recently, an elegant high-heeled pointed top boot imported from France. Some of these things may be here to stay, but most, as is the way of fashion, will vanish as quickly as snow.

The Revolution reached a climax in the little shop-ping centre of Carnaby Street which became for a while a synonym for daring modern fashion. One speciality was discarded uniforms. These had been, from the distant days of the general adoption of uniforms, (a stroke of military genius usually ascribed to Gustavus Adolphus in the seventeenth century) a customary clothing of the poor. The U-proletarians really began to look like the genuine article when they appeared in ragged and faded regimentals with unpolished buttons. Perhaps this in part accounts for the brevity of Carnaby Street's career in the late 1960s. It was all over in less than two years, after which it only enjoyed an artificial life as a tourist attraction.

As the Carnaby Street episode indicates, the revolution depended as much on revival as on innovation. One revival was inevitable. It was of that degradingly hideous fashion of the late 1920s: Oxford bags. It was applied to jeans and with the tightness of these garments over the posterior, reached heights of grotesqueness. It is still with us today but is not considered U. It was preceded by another and short-lived revival of the Edwardian and early Georgian drain-pipe trousers. In pre-war days older men had to be coaxed into wearing what seemed to them clownishly wide trousers. After 1969 they had to be coaxed back with equal difficulty into trousers of the measurements to which they had once been used.

And what about hats? Of them it may be said as was said of snakes in *The Natural History of Iceland*. Chapter 72 runs: 'Concerning snakes. There are no snakes to be met with throughout the whole island'.

The difficulty came when men took to wearing natural long hair once again. It must be remembered that this had not been done since the late 19th century, so that it is not a matter for surprise that there were no hats to fit the new fashion. The young progressives were not averse to the discordant, but long cavalier-style locks crowned by a bowler or homburg hat struck a note of absurdity far beyond what the Reformers

wanted. It followed that, except for fur caps in the
winter, hats vanished among the followers of fashion,
U and non-U. They are only worn today as part of
service uniform and by older people.

It seems that the Revolution, inaugurated about
1950, is now over. Things, as they say, have settled
down. The pattern left behind is not simple, for all the
striving of the legislators to abolish class and sex and
other irremovable objects for the sake of simplicity. As
regards the outward signs of dress and personal adorn-
ment, there is at the moment, I understand, a swing
away from the untradition of the era of rags. It is no
longer U, any more than jeans which, in old tailoring
jargon, 'woo the form' at the posterior and then flared
into Oxford bags lower down. Jeans are still worn, but
U people wear them cut to the conventional pattern.
People originally dressed in jeans as an economy measure, but that is no longer the object. To dress in jeans
according to U principles costs almost as much as to
dress in conventional suits.

The stress on tradition has led to less long hair. It
has not meant a return to the military style of 1880-1960,
but to one more like the early Victorian. The prejudice
against beards has completely vanished. Personal possessions such as one's watch, umbrella, and even one's
boots and shoes should have the look of being inherited
and not bought. Heavy luggage, obviously made before the age of air travel, is esteemed as U-luggage. In
a word, after the age of turmoil, an age of conservative
consolidation has set in.

While these movements have been going ahead, what
might collectively be known as the movement towards
polite proletarianism, comparable to the French post-
revolutionary movement towards *bourgeoisissement*,
another movement, as in those days, has been going
forward towards a new elegance. We also, in our time,

[61]

have our *incroyables*. They have most notably been responsible for a reform of evening dress, reviving frilled
shirts in the place of uniform starch and innovating
open necks. Naturally they are a very small minority,
but it is to be hoped that they will leave their mark.

It is always interesting to note, after a revolutionary
storm, the often surprising things which remain. Not
always desirable things, not always sensible things. It
was not until 1935 that the Imperial double-headed
eagles of the Kremlin were replaced by Red Stars. I was
there, on my one and only visit, when this change was
being made. At the end of the sartorial revolution
through which we have lived, we are left with the
dreary old collar and sailor knot tie for our neckwear.
They have had a needlessly long life, over a hundred
years of it, yet all efforts to displace them by lovely silk
scarves and so on have failed. It shows a weakness of the
imagination in the reformers and the hosiers of Europe
and the USA. Perhaps the Asians, once great dressers,
may be inspired to do something. The 'Nehru jacket'
was a sign of their influence. May we not look to them
again? They have put themselves out of the running
for much too long.

Another thing that has remained unchanged despite
the storm is the evening tail coat for very formal occa-
sions. Though obsolete at dances, it is still invariably
worn by the conductor of an orchestra at a concert, although its back view is painfully ill-suited to his necessary gesturing. I think it was the immortal Nat Gub-
bins's Awful Child who, in consequence of this custom,
was moved to describe thus a concert it attended: 'Then
a waiter came and tried to hit the band.' If I have a
complaint to voice about the changes I have witnessed,
it is that some of the most necessary have not gone far
enough.

'Then a waiter came and tried to hit the band'

Work: On Being Working-Class

THE EARL OF HAREWOOD
IN AN INTERVIEW

Until 1918 the profession of a peer or gentleman was to own land and look after it: his younger brothers went into the Diplomatic Corps (or, if they failed for that, the Indian Civil Service), the Army, Navy, House of Commons or Church, or read for the Bar. Some of the land they owned, especially that of Highland chieftains, was barren and worthless except for deer-stalking or grouse-shooting. From Ireland, where many adventurers had been given estates in the time of Cromwell, of Queen Elizabeth I or even earlier, they relied on strong-armed agents to extract rents from a half-starved population. There were very rare exceptions of younger sons of noble houses whom poverty had obliged to go into business, such as Andrew Drummond, a scion of one of the greatest Scottish families, who came south to seek his fortune and founded Drummond's Bank, in the early eighteenth century.

After the peace of 1918 noblemen's names began to appear as directors of City companies, adding respectability to the board and glamour to the writing-paper. This semi-professional involvement of peers may rarely have entailed hard work. It was, however, the beginning of a new life-style, and by 1939 a number of well-born men were stockbrokers. After 1945 many peers or their heirs, even those who began with perfect profiles – to quote Oscar Wilde – ended by adopting a useful profession. Some worked for choice, some from dire neces-

sity. Lord Strathnaver, heir to the Countess of Sutherland, became a Detective-Constable, CID, in the Metro-
politan Police; the Earl of Buckinghamshire was a
corporation gardener; the heir to the Earl of Essex
works in a post office; and Earl Annesley, when he succeeded, was an electrician. The late Lord Methuen and
the present Earl Haig were and are serious artists,
though they may not have lived by the sale of their
pictures. On the other hand, the Earl of Ypres, after
financial difficulties, took a job as an hotel porter, and
the 9th Lord Massy was presumably a greengrocer because he needed the money. While the Earl of Westmorland is an active director of Sotheby's, his heir Lord
Burghersh runs a night-club. Lord Newport, heir to the
Earl of Bradford, owns the Caviar Bar; Viscount St
Davids has made a business out of canal boats; the
Marquess of Queensberry is a potter and Professor of
Ceramics at the Royal College of Art; and Lord
Hesketh is a motor-racing proprietor. Born a younger
son without expectations, Lord Gerald Wellesley was a
practising architect, before the death of a nephew in
the war made him Duke of Wellington. Mr David
Somerset, heir presumptive to the Duke of Beaufort, is
an art dealer (the Marlborough Galleries), and the Earl
of Rosebery, who recently sold Mentmore, has always
had a passion for stage lighting, and set up his own business to deal in it. Lord Montagu of Beaulieu ran an
advertising agency long before he founded the famous
vintage car museum at Beaulieu; the Earl of Drogheda
edited the *Financial Times* and the Earl of Lichfield is
a high-powered and fashionable photographer.

No mention has been made – for it would be out of
place in this essay – of law lords, of new peers promoted
for excellence in some profession or for their political
services, or of Life Peers, usually intended to serve the
Socialist Party in the Upper House.

[65]

Many peers and landowners have since 1945 made a business out of opening their houses to the public, but those who did it in the most professional way, such as the Duke of Bedford, incurred at first the direst opprobrium from other members of their class. Was he justified, simply in order to pay a million or so in death duties, in installing fairgrounds, childrens' playgrounds, shopping precincts and a zoo? Most other aristocrats thought not: but Woburn prospered. To keep up beautiful Longleat, one of the few country houses on which Shakespeare can have set eyes, could the Marquess of Bath be excused for having cars parked all over the grass of his enchanted valley, so that the view from Heaven's Gate on a Sunday midday was a sea of glittering beetles? The poor man has to pay an annual bill of £15,000 for central heating alone. In 1965 he resorted to lions. This was such a success that people almost gave up visiting the Earl of Shaftesbury's neighbouring seat, the enchanting St Giles's, altogether.

The Earl of Harewood, who opened his Yorkshire house and park to the public, was slightly unusual among landowners in that his family had only acquired their property in the mid-eighteenth century; and he was unusual among peers in being the grandson of King George V. He also chose the unusual profession of musical impresario.

The Lascelles family had long been established in Yorkshire when their vastly increased fortunes, derived from West Indian sugar, enabled them to buy a great estate – quite a hard thing to do at the time, as landowners clung on to land – to build a new palace on the hill and to hire Robert Adam to design, with the benefit of their advice, its fantastic interior. A Barony and an Earldom, reasonably demanded of Pitt, followed the acquisition of land. Having built their Xanadu and planted the engirdling paradise, they did nothing more

with the benefit of their advice . . .

dramatic over the next century than attend the House of Lords, marry off their daughters and ride to hounds.

On leave in 1916 from France, where he served with exceptional courage, Harry Lascelles, heir of the 5th Earl, ran into his uncle the 2nd Marquess (and 15th Earl) of Clanricarde, who was a comparative stranger to him, at the St James's Club. The huge income of this miser and recluse was derived from an Irish estate which had been in his family for centuries. He took a fancy to his Grenadier nephew, who, like himself, was interested in works of art, and dying shortly afterwards, left him two million pounds. When Harry Lascelles found he had survived the war, be began collecting Titian, Bellini and El Greco, and married the King's daughter.

Though George, the elder son of this marriage, now 7th Earl of Harewood, still bears the onus of caring for Harewood House and its park, these now belong, in all senses but the legal, to the nation – or to anyone willing to spend a pound in order to pass a day in their purlieus. The park is a favourite place of recreation for the people of industrial Leeds and of the surrounding countryside. Few of these subscribers to its maintenance can know what its upkeep entails. (After the storms of 1962 thirty thousand new trees had to be planted.) The Bird Garden, an inspired creation of Lord Harewood's, cunningly laid out on the wooded north bank of the lake, has given pleasure to millions who never heard of Chippendale or Cima da Conegliano, and is one of the wonders of Britain.

As Managing Director of the English National Opera, based on the London Coliseum, Lord Harewood is responsible for about 500 people, including 45 principal singers, 76 chorus, 92 orchestra, 90 stage staff. There are seven main departments, Music, Stage, Production, Finance, Administration, Planning and Personnel. Each morning a report is submitted by the

Stage Manager about the previous night's performance: this may be two pages, with details such as the missing of a light cue or the non-functioning of a smoke gun. The Box Office also submits daily returns, showing how many seats were sold at each price, how many were booked in advance, how many bought on the day, and how many through 'libraries' (agencies). Harewood cannot attend every rehearsal, but hardly ever misses a dress rehearsal (usually on Monday afternoons) of the four to five new operas produced and twenty old productions revived every year. He attends three out of four performances to see changes of cast. His secretary at the theatre types about 100 letters a week, his secretary at the London house about 40 a week: most of these would have been dictated into a dictaphone at odd moments – at the week-end or during the twenty minutes before dinner. He goes abroad to hear opera, to attend congresses or to judge competitions, probably a dozen times a year. The Board meets monthly, so does the Finance and General Committee; the Opera and Marketing Committees each once a quarter. Harewood is a great believer in doing business at lunch – 'the only time you can be sure of keeping people in a good mood for an hour and a half'. There is a casting meeting followed by lunch every Wednesday; there are fortnightly lunches for the heads of departments. Soloists, conductors, producers, publishers figure in his diary at lunchtime. Lord Harewood tries to have lunch with his wife once at the beginning of the oyster season in September and once at the end in April.

Saturdays and Sundays are usually spent at Harewood. This is not just a restful week-end, as some of the estate (about 7,000 acres), with farms and forests, still remains, and what has gone has been replaced by a house-opening business which brings in over a quarter of a million visitors a year. It doesn't run itself and, though the Agent is one of Harewood's closest friends, there are frequent conferences and discussions.

When he took on the Coliseum job he thought that if the organization was functioning properly he should have 'nothing to do' except in emergencies. This, of course, didn't work out. He thinks the telephone, internal as well as external, is the bane of life, but is seldom off it.

'I decided quite early in life that I wanted to be employed in an opera house in some capacity. At six, in Yorkshire, I heard a record of the Prelude to Act I of *Die Walküre*. I began to collect records. At nine or ten I saw the film *Blossom Time*, in Harrogate, with Richard Tauber as Schubert. I think Schubert is still my favourite composer. At Eton I heard my first opera *The Marriage of Figaro*, given by a small group called the Chantecleer Opera Company. The first opera I heard at Covent Garden was *The Bartered Bride* in 1939. Then I heard *The Magic Flute* and *Butterfly*, with Joan Cross, at Sadler's Wells. When the war came I joined the Grenadier Guards, and after five months in action in Italy was taken prisoner in June 1944. In Spangenberg prison camp I read through Grove's *Dictionary of Music* (some of which I remembered), but had only got as far as S when we were moved to Colditz. After my release, in October 1945, I went as ADC to my great-uncle, Lord Athlone, who was Governor-General of Canada, and I heard Melchior in *Die Walküre* at the Met, in New York. In 1947 I went rather belatedly to Cambridge, where I read English in a desultory way, made some friends, and – mostly in London – heard a lot of music, including opera. I also discovered I wasn't a musician, only a hanger-on. On 30 July 1948 Eric Walter White of the Arts Council brought me together at lunch with Richard Buckle, who was then running the monthly magazine *Ballet*. I

the bane of life

agreed to contribute a monthly article on opera, and in October, it changed its name to *Ballet and Opera*. In 1950 *Ballet* and *Opera* became two separate magazines and I edited the latter. In 1953 I handed it over to Harold Rosenthal.'

From *Who's Who*:
... Managing Director, English National Opera since 1972; 1951–1953 a Director, Royal Opera House, Covent Garden; 1953–1960 on the staff; 1969–72, a Director; 1956–1966 Chairman, Music Advisory Committee, the British Council; 1958–1974 Artistic Director, Leeds Festival; 1961–1965 Artistic Director, Edinburgh Festival; 1963–1967 Chancellor of the University of York; 1966–1972 Chairman, Music Panel, Arts Council; 1966–1976 Artistic Adviser, New Philharmonia Orchestra; 1969–1977 Chairman, BBC Music Advisory Committee; 1962 onwards, President Leeds United Football Club; 1963–1972 President, English Football Association; English Opera Group; Rural Music Schools Association; Royal Manchester College of Music; British-Italian Society; Director, English Stage Company; Overseas Director, Australian Opera; President, Sports Fund for the Gifted ...

Lord Harewood finds that to work at least twice as hard as most men (though he would not be so boastful as to say that) is a small price to pay for having done what he wanted to do in life, like Wordsworth's Happy Warrior, and to have succeeded not only in 'being employed in an Opera House in some capacity', but in running with mastery one of the world's great companies. Being a member of the Royal Family has not made his life easier – rather the contrary; he has met with opposition and active discouragement from members of his own class. Yet, to his sacking by Edinburgh when a divorce from his first wife was imminent and to his being passed over by Covent Garden after the death of David Webster we owe the present glory of the ENO, a people's opera in the highest sense, and one which has put the more highly subsidized Royal Opera House in the shade.

As a new member of the working class, however, Harewood has had his share of troubles with the striking class.

'In the commercial theatre, if the cast of a play went on strike, the show would close and the actors would be automatically out of work. The English National Opera is non-profit making and has no shareholders – except, in a sense, the public; and in effect it cannot give notice to its employees. There are three unions involved, the Musicians' Union, which causes the least trouble, Equity (representing the singers) and NATTKE (stage hands and electricians). Knowing that the Board cannot close the theatre down if unions choose to 'work to rule', troublemakers bank on our subsidized company being baled out by the Arts Council (*i.e.* the Treasury). Almost any point or part of a point gained by the unions ensures a lowering of standards: less time spent on perfecting productions, fewer operas, poorer quality.'

The Press have come to take Lord Harewood seriously, recognizing a hard-worker who delivers the goods; fellow musicians know there is no greater professional in the business; friends are continually abashed by his modesty and self-effacement. If never to claim credit is one sign of a gentleman a hundred illustrations could be given of Harewood's nobility. Let one suffice.

In the 'fifties, when he worked at Covent Garden, Harewood constantly urged the Board to revive Donizetti's *Lucia* for a certain young soprano in the company, who had already sung Pamina, Gilda and Desdemona, but whose rare gift for *coloratura* had never been revealed. Again and again the Board objected that nobody would listen to Donizetti in this day and age, that *coloratura* was a thing of the past and that Harewood was exaggerating the genius of the girl in question. At last, when some other production fell through, they gave in and took his advice. On the evening Joan Sutherland triumphed in *Lucia*, to become world-famous overnight, Harewood could not get out of an invitation to Buckingham Palace, so missed all the fun. When a friend heard this story, years later, he exclaimed 'How grateful to you she must have been!' 'Oh, she never knew,' said Lord Harewood.

Not Quite a Gentleman

RICHARD BUCKLE

'WHO ARE THEY, DARLING?'

Some years ago my Aunt Violet and I were discussing
her first cousin H., and Violet said: 'H. is an awful
snob. She's always saying "Who *are* they, darling?" '
I realized that I was being vaguely warned, and that the
mysterious 'they' were people like Buckles. It struck me
in a flash that snobbery, which is supposed to be the
behaviour of inferior people apeing or trying to get to
know their 'betters', was also an attribute of people in
the highest rank of society, for Cousin H. was the
daughter of a duke, the half-sister of a duke, the widow
of a duke, the mother of two dukes and the mother-in-
law of two more.

Well, who *are* they, anyway, darling? I am jolly well
going to tell you who one at least of the wretched out-
siders is. This is the case history of someone who is not
quite a gentleman, who has never quite known how to
behave, who is definitely not a social success, and who
has been much disliked by some of the best people.

NOT QUITE A GENTLEMAN

Everyone has thirty-two great-great-great-grandparents
(except when some of them are the same people, as happens particularly with inbred Royalty). If, by some
extraordinary chance mine had all been assembled under the same roof in London around 1800 and numbered
1 to 32 (No. 1 being my father's father's father's father's
father and No. 32 my mother's mother's mother's

Everyone has thirty-two great-great-great-grandparents

mother's mother), most of those from 17 to 32 would have known each other. Nos. 1 to 8 would have passed muster, but Nos. 9 to 16 would have been conspicuous by their Devonshire or Westmorland accents and calloused workers' hands. If anyone should ask 'Why on earth is Dicky Buckle editing a book on U and non-U?' – and he may well ask, for I was even left out of *Debrett* when my grandmother Sandford died* – the answer is that I come from such a mixture of upper-, middle-, and lower-class families that I think I have exceptional qualifications.

1 and 3 were brothers, so their children were first cousins and I have a double dose of Buckle blood. (The chief Buckle characteristic is to take no nonsense from superiors – which is hardly the best way to get on in the world.) 8 came from the family of William Harvey, who discovered the circulation of the blood. 9 was a farmer. 13 was a miller. 21's Anglo-Irish mother was seventh cousin to George Washington. 22 was a daughter of the Prime Minister Duke of Portland. 23, a banker, was descended from King Charles II and Nell Gwynn. 24 was Welsh, so presumably descended from a dragon. 25, another descendant of King Charles II (by Louise de Kéroualle), was the man of whom the tart Harriette Wilson wrote: 'I shall not say why or how I became, at the age of fifteen, the mistress of the Earl of Craven'. 26 was an actress. 27 was brother-in-law to King George IV, though his Catholic sister's marriage was not acknowledged. 32 was granddaughter of the 8th Earl of Strathmore, whose wife's grandfather had been a shoemaker.

It was my grandmother Sandford who was always using the expression 'He's not quite a gentleman'; and she would sometimes add thoughtfully 'You could ask

* Though, at the time of writing, straining every nerve in the effort to get back in again.

him to luncheon, but not to dinner.' This applied to lawyers or doctors. My grandmother Buckle's father was a doctor, though descended from Devonshire farmers as far as the genealogist's eye can reach. (A little money had helped him to get more education outside Devonshire. He may have been the first Turner ever to leave the county.)

Nothing will illustrate better my mixed heredity than to contrast my two grandmothers. (Both married soldiers, and my father was a soldier too.) My widowed grandmother Sandford (born Craven) sat on a sofa in her Paddington flat doing 'work', that is, *petit point*, with a small dog gnawing a gold bangle on a cushion at her feet. Lawyers and doctors were not the only people she called 'common'. Of a former butler whom she accused – without appearing particularly to blame him – of killing her husband by smuggling into the house bottles of forbidden drink, she commented 'Such a *common* man!'; and I wondered what impossible degree of distinction she demanded in upper servants. Her Sandford sisters-in-law were 'common, *dirty* women' and her mother-in-law, whom I just remember, was 'a common, *mean* old woman!' Great-grandma Sandford, rather well-off, was doubtless tight-fisted where the *soignée* but extravagant Connie was concerned, but she was a Greville and had many distinguished ancestors. In calling her 'common' Connie Sandford meant 'plain, dull, unsmart and not an asset in society.' Connie and her mother-in-law each had a sister who married a Duke of Richmond, though Aunt Isobel did not live to become a duchess.

My grandmother Buckle, Dr Turner's daughter, had married a gentleman – if you can call a man descended from a Lord Mayor who was granted arms in 1594 a gentleman – but she used the expression 'going to Town', said 'gurl' instead of 'gairl', gushed, and talked to strangers in railway carriages. She was mad about God, butterflies and holding forth to a captive audience over tea in the garden. The best book she wrote was about dying soldiers whom she tended at Netley Hospital during the 1914 war. She was so sympathetic – except to upper-class women like my other grandmother – that people she talked to in trains sometimes became her friends for life.

As a boy I soon realized I could curry favour and raise a laugh by describing one grandmother to another, thus qualifying as a toady and lickspittle. I don't think, however, I relayed to Granny Buckle the following conversation with my Sandford grandmother, or she would have dropped dead. 'You sow your wild oats, darling.' 'What *do* you mean?' 'It's very important for you to get to know things. I'd much rather marry an immoral man than a moral one.' 'Why?' 'Because they know the ropes and they don't maul you about so.'

Granny Buckle always watched anxiously for signs of my pleasure-loving, spendthrift 'Craven side' coming out; and Grandmother Sandford attributed all my awkwardness and vulgarity to the Turners and Buckles.

LEARNING THE FORM

From my mother, the only parent available, I picked up the basic principles of how not to be intolerable: not to smell, not to fidget (to this day the sight of someone sitting cross-legged and waggling his foot drives me mad), not to close in on the person you are talking to, not to eat chocolates in the theatre. You only wore a ring on the little finger of your left hand, if at all; you left undone the bottom waistcoat button; it was too frightful to have a matching tie and handkerchief; and if you wore an open shirt (with the intention of playing some game) you didn't spread it neatly over the collar of your coat. To stress the first syllable in 'September' or the last in 'Sandhurst' was unforgivable. My mother laughed at me for pronouncing 'poetry' as it is written, but I have seldom heard anyone else say 'poytry'. Great-grandma Sandford, I was told, had said 'yaller', 'cup o' tay' and 'spittacles'. When her daughter, my great-aunt Dolly, caught me saying 'gurl' instead of 'gairl' she announced that she would give half-a-crown a month if I promised on my honour to forfeit threepence ('thrippence') every time I slipped up. I was soon cured, but the allowance (known as 'Rabbits' because it came on the first of the month) continued, slightly increased, even when I was an officer in the army on active service.

From my grandmother Sandford I learned that paying compliments was vulgar. From her brother, my great-uncle Caryl Craven, I learned that one doesn't 'take' anything except 'med'sin'. His fury at me for putting a log on the fire instead of ringing the bell has not born much fruit in later life, because nowadays I would ring in vain.

My grandfather Buckle, a retired General, was my only other male relation, and I think in some ways he was a perfect gentleman. He thought nothing of birth, treated everyone equally, hunted (until 1914), shot and worked in the garden. From him I learned that 'When a hedge or fence you cross,/Though of time it prove a loss,/From your gun the cartridge take ...' and all that gun lore. He also taught me to acknowledge money by return of post.

At Oxford I discovered that it was not done to refer to New College as 'New' – it does give one shivers for some reason –, though, of course, it would be unthinkable to pronounce the word 'college' after the name of any other. When war came and I scraped into the Scots Guards we were lectured on what not to do or say (on the assumption that as temporary gentlemen we must be utter freaks, like the young actor – now famous – who, when asked by the Lieutenant-Colonel Commanding the Grenadiers what he had done in peacetime, replied 'I was in rep'). I knew that you said 'in the Coldstream', not 'in the Coldstreams'; and the only unfamiliar prohibition concerned the carrying of parcels.

In the 1940s I came to know through my friend Jean Hugo what importance the French attached to '*place à table*' (not '*placement*' as the English say) and to going through doors last.

With all this knowledge I should have been equipped to face the world.

HOW NOT TO GET ON IN SOCIETY

My father was killed in 1918, and left my mother very hard up. This laid her open to the reminder that she should never have married him in the first place. (No marriage of any of my ancestors for the last hundred years has been approved of by either side. Nobody ever thought anybody was good enough.) My mother gave me the best education possible on the least possible money, and I went to Marlborough as my father had done, and got in on the cheap. I therefore missed Eton and meeting people who would be 'friends for life.' Marlborough was definitely for the sons of clergymen, professional men and the poorer gentry, and could therefore be called middle-class, though it has turned out such bright stars as William Morris and the present Poet Laureate.* Friendship with Derek Hill (now a celebrated landscape and portrait painter) proved fatal. He taught me the facts of life, which went to my head. Not only did I become an 'aesthete', with all that that implied, I plunged into the epidemic 'isms' of the 'thirties – atheism, pacifism, socialism. My *dégringolade*

* Sir John Betjeman. Author of the poem 'How to get on in Society', printed by Nancy Mitford in *Noblesse Oblige* (Hamish Hamilton, 1956).

[81]

from grace can be charted in the surviving letters of poor Granny Buckle. In one she expresses interest in some book which has recently inflamed me, and says my grandfather wishes to read it before giving his opinion on my plan to turn Moslem. I resigned from the Officers' Training Corps, refused to wear a dinner-jacket or go to dances and wouldn't stand up for 'God Save the King'. The pacifism had no effect on my behaviour when war was declared, as I was too afraid to offend my grandfather not to join up at once: but the temporary socialism was enough to alienate my great-uncle Caryl Craven, who left all his possessions to the richest of his six nieces (Duchess H, mentioned above).

After the war I knew no one in London, and my fellow-officer, Iain Moncreiffe, the kindest of men, tried to introduce me to people. (A vivid memory of this period is the sight of Lady Cunard's pretty bottom – we had walked into her suite at the Dorchester, gone through several open doors, calling out, and caught her in front of the bedroom looking-glass, powdering her face, with her nightgown hitched up behind.) It was no good. Being shy, I was always ill at ease at parties, and either shut up like a clam or, emboldened by drink, said all the wrong things. I could hear myself doing it. I could even see people disliking me across the room before they met me. My voice may have been off-putting too – it's too fruity and highly coloured, and I don't know where it came from: but I can't change it now. General Mossolov, a courtier of the last Tsar, described in his memoirs how you could always tell who the genuine aristocrats were at a Court ball by their air of being at home anywhere. I wasn't.

Fatal not to be rich, fatal not to go to Eton, fatal not to hunt and like horses. Even those pampered quadrupeds could spot a mile off that I was not out of the top drawer. Well, to hell with horses.

before giving his opinion on my plan to turn Moslem

WHAT DOES HE DO?

I made a disastrous choice of profession. Business has become respectable and stockbroking almost *chic*. But I became a ballet critic, which is barely legal in this country between consenting adults.

I realized my mistake too late. The description of two encounters, nearly a quarter of a century apart, will illustrate my changed attitude towards this chosen profession. In spring 1945, when my soldiering in Italy was almost over, Henry of Bavaria took me to tea with Berenson at Settignano. The great man asked me 'What did you do before the war?'; and I, who had barely burst into print in 1939, answered proudly 'I'm a ballet critic.' Berenson was amazed and went into an aria about the infinite subdivisions of human activity. In 1967 a great friend, June Churchill, asked me to her daughter's coming-out ball. I loathe dances, but I went, and dined first with Mrs Ian Fleming. After dinner I suddenly found myself alone in the drawing-room with Randolph Churchill, who was obviously in a truculent mood. 'Who *are* you? What do you do?' he barked at me across the room. I should have answered (Alas! *l'esprit d'escalier*) 'I'm a hack journalist like yourself' or 'I'm your wife's lover', but politeness prevailed. 'I write about ballet in the *Sunday Times*'. I felt such a bloody fool. By then I was ashamed of my trade.

THE LAST STRAW

No, I was not a social success, nor did I ever really set out to be one. I never gate-crashed a party nor fished for invitations; and often, when I had accepted an invitation, did not turn up. In that sense I was no snob. Yet I got the reputation of being one because of my interest in genealogy.

[84]

The joys of genealogy are not really essentially snobbish: they are allied to those of the detective and the
collector. The genealogist in his search for completeness
links up mankind. To follow the roots of a family tree
into the dark earth of history is at once an aesthetic, a
moral, and a patriotic pleasure. I well remember my
shock of delight when I discovered, in the Bodleian
Library, that I was descended from Nell Gwynn; I am
proud too of my devil-may-care ancestor Surrey the
poet, who was executed for snobbery in 1547; and when
I read the first line of Shakespeare's first sonnet, in which
he begs the young Southampton to get married and
beget a posterity, I am glad that of that posterity, for
better or worse, I make one. Our obscurer ancestors are
just as much fun, and far more difficult to trace. Some
years ago I enlisted the aid of a renowned West Country
genealogist to do some researches on Granny Buckle's
farming forebears in Devonshire, but I think that after
a sensational start he must have run into difficulties or
lost interest. Will Mr Hugh Peskett kindly answer my
last letter of 3 January 1969?

The thing to remember about genealogy is never, unless you are Iain Moncreiffe, to refer to your own forebears either in print or in conversation. Common people
resent your having ancestors, and magnates are incredu-
lous that you should lay claim to any. The briefest mention of King Henry VII can be used by people who want
to make mischief as proof that you are a snob. Never
claim kinship with those in a more elevated station
than yourself. Let them do it first.

ALL PASSION SPENT

Now that I have given up ballet criticism, London,
drink and going out in society, I think I may be on the
way to respectability at last. Pottering ineffectually

along the dock-lined paths of my Wiltshire garden, I contemplate with senile shamelessness a life of social disaster; and as the last rays of a dying sun tinges the dead elms, I go indoors to twiddle the well-thumbed knobs of my trusty television.

How delightful it is that Education for All should have resulted in universal ignorance! Night after night I observe on television our rulers, our idols and our trend-setters getting everything wrong. Few can frame or finish a simple sentence. A noted newscastress pronounces 'duchess' with an accent on the second syllable. How is it I know and she doesn't that while the 'ess' in 'princess' is sounded, in 'duchess' and 'countess' it is not? She has learnt that the 'er' in 'Hertfordshire', like that in 'Derby', is pronounced 'ar', but she still makes two mistakes in the same word, pronouncing the 't' and saying 'sheer' instead of 'sh'r'. She goes on to pronounce 'Norwich' as 'Norritch', instead of 'Norridge'. For the fiftieth time this week I hear about 'negosiations in Rhodeessia' instead of 'negoshiations in Rhodeesher'. (Even the *Oxford Dictionary* bears me out on that one.) The Deputy Editor of *The Times* accents the last syllable of 'composite', instead of the first, making it rhyme with 'fight'. Mrs Thatcher, who may or may not be our next Prime Minister, pronounces 'involved' with a long 'o', as in 'vote'.

I wonder if it would do any good to adopt the tactics of my dear great-aunt and godmother, Dolly Sandford, and try giving Mrs Thatcher a small allowance, payable on the first day of every month?

Dear Mrs Thatcher

Would you allow a well-meaning old soul to offer you half-a-crown a month on the understanding that you are on your honour, every time you pronounce 'involved' incorrectly, to forfeit threepence (pronounced 'thrippence') . . .

THEN, SUDDENLY, LOVE DAWNED ...

The preceding notes on telecast mispronunciations –
and hundreds more – were made during February and
March 1978, for I took my duties as an editor seriously,
and it had been at the end of January that Mr Brooks-
Baker, Managing Director of Debrett's, employed me
to stir up class hatred in Great Britain and Northern
Ireland.

Then, late in the evening of 30 April, I turned on
the television to see an attractive woman – though she
was about my age – talking in the most natural and
amusing way about life and politics. Her pronunciation
was impeccable, and she was witty without apparently
trying to be. The programme included clips from older
films of her lectures to Californian undergraduates, and
I could see that she was a marvellous public speaker.
Though she never seemed to be making a point, when
she *did*, and her audience exploded into laughter, she
would pause, look down at her notes, and go on in the
same even manner as before. I was bowled over. Love
was born.

This divine creature had been a member of the Communist Party, but left it because of the bloody-minded-
ness of Moscow. She had, however, continued to work for
Civil Rights. Although English, she was married *en
secondes noces* to an American. Her knowledge, wit, style
and sense had been acquired without 'the benefits of
education': for she had never been to school. Her name
was Jessica Mitford. She, Diana and Unity were three
sisters that I had never met. I had known Jessica's first
husband, Esmond Romilly. Now, she was married again.

I remembered, years ago, sitting next to Jessica's
cousin, Lady Beit, at dinner in Ireland. (If Clemmie
Beit – a posthumous child, for her father was killed in
the first war – had been born a boy, the famous Mitford

sisters would never have been Hons at all.) Lady Beit said 'Mitfords always fall in love with *peculiar men.*' It is hardly 'my place' to enlarge upon this theme. One might have added that they – Mitford girls – often married millionaires. I considered my rival, Jessica Mitford's present husband. He was of Polish-Jewish descent and a university professor, probably a bit younger and certainly much better paid than myself, even if not, perhaps, a millionaire. I watched them having tea in California with a friendly black couple, and noticed that nobody flinched when Jessica said 'When I was a gairl ...' I weighed my chances. *I* was a 'peculiar man.'

If you wish to follow the sequel of a true love story more thrilling even than the fantastic fictions of Nancy Mitford, look out for *On a cycle through the Rockies,* to be published by Debrett's in the near future. . . .

The Expectancy and Rose
of the Fair State

SIR IAIN MONCREIFFE OF THAT ILK, BART.
CHIEF OF THE CLAN MONCREIFFE

It was pitch dark. We were cold, wet and uncomfortable. I had been blown up by a shell, punctured a bit by shrapnel, ignominiously crushed by a dislodged boulder, and could only limp at a crawl while my soldier servant Guardsman Fraser carried my equipment. So I had remained behind on the mountainside at midnight with our patrol officer Dicky Buckle and his rear party, who were laying mines on the goat track to cover the Brigade's withdrawal. We weren't sure how close the enemy were on our heels. It was the end of the first (unsuccessful) battle of Monte Camino, now a battle honour on the Colours. We were the last on 'the Hill', a fine moment, we felt, in regimental history. Naturally, therefore, we were discussing heraldry.

Having established the basic fact that the Buckles were fairly nouveau, springing from an Elizabethan burgher who was Lord Mayor of London, we had got on to considering the ninety-four quarterings that Dicky had inherited on his mother's side. These were quite impressive. I recollect that we had reached the exact point when he said:

"I quarter Hoo."

"Who?" I replied, mishearing him in mental transliteration.

"Hoo".

[89]

"Yes, but who?"

"Hoo", Dicky went on hooting like an owl.

Suddenly it dawned on me that he meant the simple *argent & sable* coat of the mediaeval Lord Hoo of Hoo, an unpopular Knight of the Garter much derided in song by the revolting peasantry at the time of Jack Cade's rebellion. This exact moment remains fixed in my mind, as we were recalled to our rather macabre modern surroundings by a loud explosion followed by yells mingled with oaths. One of the mines we'd just laid had claimed their first victim.

Now, politeness apart, the true U reaction to the information that Dicky quartered the arms of this obscure mediaeval peer would either be boredom or interest. So too would doubtless be the reaction of most ordinary people. But a standard non-U reaction would be to resent him and feel he needed "taking down a peg" for "showing off". The middle classes, perhaps sensing some outflanking Jones, would raise their plaintive bleat: "Who does he think he is?" I well remember a peer, giving a public lecture about his stately home, mentioning (for it was relevant) that he descended from King Charles II. The non-U female next to me turned in typical misunderstanding to express her shock at such conceit. Her Pavlov-bitch comment ended resentfully: "I *descend* – Period."

This is a succinct form of the standard non-U crack, when any forebears are mentioned, that "we all descend from Adam." The funny thing about most of the people who make it, is that few of them realise it's actually true. Biologists, when prodded hard enough, have to admit that every man who has ever lived since the world began has inherited his Y chromosome (the genetic factor that makes him a man) from the same single humanoid being, just one person who lived at a particular moment long long ago – however he in turn was evolved. The

"Who?" "Hoo."

biologists dislike admitting this even more, when it's pointed out that we had a convenient name for this being even before my coz Darwin postulated him. For *adam* is simply a very ancient Mesopotamian word meaning Man. And, as I've written elsewhere, to the similar crack

> *When Adam delved, and Eve span,*
> *Who then was gentleman?*

I always reply 'Adam. How could it have been Eve?'

In Adam, therefore, we have the embryo gentleman. But just as from the original equidae there evolved race-horses and cobs and cart-horses for different purposes, so too it has been with mankind – though fortunately we are continually crossbred.

Meanwhile, a moment's reflection will show that even had we all remained in an egalitarian Garden of Eden like lilies of the field, toiling not nor spinning, some of you would have evolved into nature's gentle men, and other of us into natural boors. For, whenever the brotherhood of man is mostly loudly proclaimed today, one would have to be pretty tone-deaf not to hear the primaeval voice of Cain.

This jealousy of our more fortunate or distinguished brethren, and especially of their children, is the deepest stain that marks out the present day as the Age of Envy. It's rather ungentlemanly, to say the least: and hardly brotherly love.

Owing to the crossbreeding that has kept mankind inter-related throughout the aeons, we've all had fore-fathers of every rank whether we can trace them or not. The most recent serf from whom I can personally trace my descent was freed by the Bishop of Zagreb in 1552: the most recent king from whom I can do the same died exactly ten years earlier. We shouldn't look down on those rude forefathers of the hamlet, without whose romps in the hay we could never have been born. But it ill becomes us also not to look up to the achievements of those grander forebears who led our nations upwards, and who evolved polite codes of conduct – courtesy means the manners of the Court – that weren't always honoured only in the breach. Nevertheless, 'the boast of heraldry' aptly sums up the poet's distaste for overdoing it.

In fact, therefore, everybody has as many ancestors as everybody else. No family is older than any other. We weren't each evolved separately like Pooh-Bah from some different personal amoeba or primordial protoplasm. It's simply that some families have maintained a known position, and their doings have been recorded longer than those of others. The Sackvilles of Buckhurst, for example, are the only Norman family who can actually prove that they were *not* at the battle of Hastings. But 'the 14th Mr Wilson' (to recall the 14th Earl of Home's famous retort when quizzed about a fellow Prime Minister) cannot prove that his direct male line ancestor wasn't one of the leaders in that battle. All the same, most people assume that descents that can't be established aren't likely to be distinguished.

As a result, U people in England – except among the tiny group of interbred ancient Catholic families like the Stourtons and Berkeleys – have an unease of discussing family history unless quite sure they are among themselves. They don't want inadvertently to make some middle-class worthy of uncertain pedigree, who might chance to be present, feel out of it. On the Continent, indeed, grand pedigrees and family histories tend to be limited to a fairly well-defined aristocratic group. But in England, precisely because the division between U and non-U is so blurred, and can so easily be crossed, delicacy imposes discretion.

In Scotland, of course, there is no such inhibition

'the boast of heraldry'

about discussing ancestry. This is for two reasons. First, we are so small a country that everybody can know who everybody else is, and there's neither need nor opportunity to pretend. But secondly, and this is a Good Thing, our noble clannish traditions are divided vertically between Names, not horizontally between classes. Campbells or Grahams may be dukes or dustmen, but they all share the same Roots, have their own special tartan and historic tradition. Moreover this is often demonstrable in practice as well as in principle. For instance, my late wife, as Countess of Erroll in her own right, was Chief of the Hays and thoroughly imbued with Hay tradition. But so equally was Mr Hay, the (unpaid) cox of the Fraserburgh lifeboat. He told me that when he joined the Royal Navy as an ordinary seaman, his father had reminded him that his forefathers had served before the mast in every generation since before Trafalgar and that, while ever mindful of the traditions of the Service, he must never forget that that he was a Hay and always live up to the great traditions of his Name. His first nautical ancestor had been an impoverished eighteenth-century cadet of the Hays of Rannes, and I could trace his line back without difficulty to a Hay baron of the thirteenth century. Here *noblesse oblige* was visibly at work in its most classless Scottish sense. Such collective nobiliary tradition is nowadays expressed particularly through the numerous and flourishing clan societies.

To revert to the contrast between the English and the Continental ideas of U, great confusion arises because a foreigner uses the word 'noble' to mean an *untitled* gentleman of known ancestry, whereas the English use the same word to mean only a Peer of the Realm and his immediate titled relations. Few English people therefore understand what is meant when it's explained that Napoleone Buonaparte was a noble by birth. Toqueville (by the way, my French friends have always told me it's non-U to refer to anybody as 'de' unless you use a prefix, *e.g.* you can refer to Monsieur de Monbrison, Amaury de Monbrison, or plain Monbrison, but never just to 'de Monbrison') observed that, as the position of a French untitled noble was fixed and unchangeable, they could know whom they pleased; but as the position of an English gentleman was judged rather by his way of life, Englishmen were anxious to avoid meeting the wrong sort of people and getting ranked with them by association.

On the Continent, apart from the Church, the upper class of noble gentlemen were expected to serve the Crown, for instance in the Army or Navy or in diplomacy, rather than engage in commerce for their own benefit: and indeed were only modestly paid but long freed from taxation as a result. Originally the knightly families holding manorial estates, the immemorial *uradel*, they were reinforced over the centuries by statesmen, by commanders in war (the *noblesse d'épée*) and by parliamentarians and judges (the *noblesse de la robe*). However, the great cities of Italy and the Empire produced patrician families of equivalent status; and grand banking families like the Medici and the Fuggers attained princely rank. But always the concept existed abroad of the legally identifiable gentleman.

In England, similar considerations applied only to the extent that in my youth, if a gentleman already had enough money, he was expected on the whole to enter the armed services or the Diplomatic Service for modest pay, otherwise the Church or the Law, and only commerce on the grand scale, with a bias in that case in favour of merchant banking. And there was always too the Empire, to go out and govern. But trade followed the flag. Though Napoleon was mauled by what he called the English leopards, he summed them up in his famous epigram as 'a nation of shopkeepers'. It is of the essence, however, that the English are romantic shopkeepers, at their best in war. So the English gentleman came to differ widely from his Continental counterpart, although every gentleman was still a potential officer in war or a potential justice of the peace, in that he was not demeaned by engaging in commerce for his own benefit – so long as he behaved like a gentleman. And in time, an able man could rise to become a gentleman by his way of life. For though it's no longer birth alone that counts, still less is it wealth alone, but rather certain indefinable attitudes of mind that go with the gentlemanly concept.

On the other hand, it would be idle to pretend that birth and at least a modicum of wealth are not a head start. If it wasn't so, there would soon be nothing much to emulate. Obviously excellent heredity combined with excellent environment tends to give good results. Without an élite, or if the élite had been deliberately held back by egalitarianism, we would never have left the caves. When a man dies in primitive New Guinea, his hut is burned and his cooking pots smashed, because his children already have huts and cooking pots of their own: as it were primitive council houses. By this 100% Capital Transfer Tax they are safely held back to the lowest common denominator even more firmly than we are going to be after a generation or two of (say) 60% CTT. Meanwhile, however, we still have some gentlemen of ancient birth with the freedom to speak their minds that goes with private means.

Within these limits there's great scope for teasing. If the Duke of Westminster, head of the house of Grosvenor, is a multi-millionaire grandee of impeccable Norman lineage, it's possible to trump him by producing a Scrope. The head of the equally ancient Norman house of Scrope is the squire of Danby. But in 1385

[97]

their positions were reversed. Sir Robert Grosvenor was a simple Cheshire knight. Lord Scrope was Lord High Chancellor of England. They came up here to bash us Scots, and started a rival row instead because they found themselves both wearing the same coat of arms: *Azure a bend Or* (a golden diagonal band on a blue field). The celebrated case of Scrope v. Grosvenor in the Court of Chivalry went on for five years. Everybody sided with the great Lord Scrope against this obscure Grosvenor knight. It was pointed out that although one of them, a Chief Justice, had been put into a legal career ('mis a la ley'), the Scropes had been 'graundes gentilhommes et de noblez' since the Conquest. The poet Chaucer, Harry 'Hotspur' and Henry of Bolingbroke (afterwards King Henry IV), all gave evidence for the Scropes.

Eventually the Lord High Constable gave judgement in favour of Lord Scrope. When Grosvenor appealed to King Richard II, he was told he had lost and must change his coat-of-arms to a wheatsheaf (now well-known to clients of the National Westminster Bank). The Grosvenors never forgot their lost *bend Or*, and after the 1st Duke of Westminster won the Derby in 1880 with his racehorse Bend Or, his grandson and heir was nicknamed 'Bend Or'. As 'Bend Or' Westminster he was recommended for a Victoria Cross in the First World War.

Meanwhile, the Scropes had refused to change their religion at the Reformation, so had been banned for centuries as Roman Catholics from all office and preferment, and their peerages had gone into abeyance among co-heiresses. The head of the family is still lord of the manor of Danby, which they inherited during the Wars of the Roses. He is Major Scrope and the Duke of Westminster is the Duke of Westminster, yet in the inner U world he still commands a special respect. People no longer wear coats-of-arms over their armour. But the

Scropes still have the last laugh. They wear a special family tie: Blue with diagonal gold bands – *Azure a bend Or*. Lady Leonora Grosvenor and Miss Diana Scrope have both stayed with me at Easter Moncreiffe simultaneously without a fracas. But Victor Grosvenor of the Life Guards, definitely a Hon. out of Nancy Mitford's Hons cupboard, has given me a standing order to find a very small Scrope for him to bash.

This brings us to Nancy Mitford's original article on 'The English Aristocracy' in *Noblesse Oblige*, and Evelyn Waugh's 'Open Letter' in reply to it, that caused such a furore some twenty years ago. The fuss was primarily because it drew attention to Professor Alan Ross's work as a philologist, in which, as a professional observer, he had noted the linguistic demarcation of upper-class English, for which he coined the abbreviation U as opposed to non-U. This work, while of natural interest to his fellow philologists, was perhaps rather embarrassing when publicised socially through no fault of his. It only made U people self-conscious when talking naturally in the way to which they'd always been accustomed, and could obviously hurt or at least irritate non-U people.

It's rather like our perennial problem in Scotland. Most, but not all, U people in Scotland speak in the accents, use the expressions, and behave in the ways, described as U by Professor Ross. They don't do this by affectation, but because it's the way their parents talked before them. The Scottish aristocracy have in fact always tended to speak the language of the political centre. My own forebears have almost certainly lived here at Moncreiffe since Pictish times, although we only assumed the surname from our lands some seven or eight centuries ago. By the end of the Dark Ages they spoke Gaelic (Moncreiffe is the Old Gaelic place-name Monadh Craoibhe), then at the Court of St Margaret perhaps briefly Anglo-Saxon. During the Scottish War of Independence in the twelve and thirteen hundreds they spoke Norman-French. (Whatever languages they spoke to their followers – Welsh or Northumbrian or Gaelic – if Wallace and Bruce met they talked to each other in Norman-French.) From the fifteenth century onwards my forefathers spake Court Scots; but after the Union, with the move of the political centre from Edinburgh to London, they gradually came to speak what Professor Ross defines as U English.

This is, of course, nothing like the accent or mode of speech of the Elizabethan English courtiers, which doubtless survives in some of the Southern States of the USA. It has, instead, been evolved collectively by the U British since the Union. People aren't surprised that Lord Devon doesn't nowadays speak broad Devonshire, nor the Duke of Norfolk with a Norfolk accent, yet they are somewhat surprised that Lord Glasgow doesn't use a glottal stop and say 'Hoots mon'. On the other hand, the situation would doubtless change naturally once again after a generation of Home Rule.

I myself, however, don't want to get involved in any embarrasing U-pontifications, except to support the well-known quip: 'If it's me it's U.' This is a modern version of the famous remark by a sixteenth-century highland chief misplaced by his host: 'Wherever Macdonald is sitting, that is the head of the table'. Earlier in this book, Professor Ross has brought readers up-to-date with U speech today, and the other contributors have described U life so much better than the What the Butler Saw sort of peeps we get from non-U playwrights and novelists. Lord Harewood in particular serves to remind us that most U people work just as hard as most other classes, differing principally only perhaps in outlook, and of course rather harder than those who have the 'right' to strike. The principal workaday U feature,

I rather think, is that off duty all ages tend to converse naturally and associate in their homes and clubs without undue regard to age or position, whereas the urban middle classes tend to move in the same age group and income group from the cradle to the grave. I noticed this especially when I was ADC to a U general and attaché to a U ambassador. But it's only the gossip columnists who pretend that aristocratic life is one unending holiday – which is no doubt what many of their readers (vicariously but mistakenly) would like their own lives to be.

When she was preparing her celebrated article on 'The English Aristocracy', Mrs Peter Rodd, better known as Nancy Mitford, asked me if I would help her over points of fact, as she was in Paris most of the time. Her questions shewed a desire to be thorough. She wanted to know how many peers had been divorced? About one in eight. How many living peers had done well in the War? She obviously meant any war: Lord Dunmore, for example, had won his Victoria Cross in 1897 but was still alive. Taking all living peers of all ages, apart from peeresses in their own right and minors, nearly a quarter had either been mentioned in despatches or decorated in battle. How many peers were Roman Catholics? I telephoned to Lord Mowbray. He asked if I included Irish peers; we settled for members of the House of Lords only; he looked in the Catholic Directory; the answer was 47. How many peers were patrons of livings? I hadn't the foggiest idea. And so on.

Perhaps her most interesting question was, how many peers really belonged to old families? This was interesting because I was surprised by the answer as it unfolded. For I discovered that well over a third of our hereditary peerage still belonged to families that had borne arms in the direct male line since the Middle Ages. So I was rather pleased when Evelyn Waugh, in his excellent

Open Letter to Nancy Mitford, wrote: 'You say that 382 peers have arms granted before 1485 *and have inherited them in the male line* . . . The statement staggers me'. But then I was distinctly miffed, if that's the right word, when he went on to suggest that her adviser had overlooked the passage of old names through heiresses to new husbands' families: 'I think you should have questioned your pursuivant more closely before accepting his figures'. I didn't know him well enough in those days to ask him not to teach his grandmother to suck eggs, and indeed always had a special respect for his brilliance as an observer of contemporary life. But I did know enough, for example, to realise that the ancestor of the present Noel earls of Gainsborough in 1485 was not a Noel, but the Red Douglas in person, or that in the male line Lord Eglinton is a Wintoun and not a Montgomerie, or that Lord De La Warr is a West and not a Sackville. The real reason for the surprisingly high number is that, almost without exception, the peers of Scotland help to swell this pre-1485 category.

Eventually, Nancy Mitford sent me her typescript. She didn't, nevertheless, accept any of my criticisms of it, some of which followed the lines of Evelyn Waugh's later Open Letter. She seemed to me to compound the different muddled misusages of the words 'noble' and 'aristocrat'; and then to link them to the ridiculous notion that they applied only and automatically to all peers. She set so much store by the courtesy style of Hon., dependent on the title conferred on her grandfather in 1902, as though she was very nouveau *noblesse de la robe*; when all the time she was immemorially *uradel*, descended in the direct male line from the mediaeval Mitfords of Mitford (what the Austrians would call *zu* Mitford and the Scots Mitford of that Ilk) whose beautifully simple coat was, and is, *Argent a fesse between three moles Sable*. Her forefather, Sir John

Mitford of Mitford, was Knight of the Shire for North-umberland in 1369, and a later Mitford of Mitford fell at the battle of Towton in the Wars of the Roses. How could she have thought that her old mediaeval aristo-cratic family were made into aristocrats by getting a bit of paper from Edward VII? Sir Percy Blakeney would have turned in his grave.

Evelyn Waugh put the true situation snob-wise very well: 'the basic principle of English social life is that *everyone* (everyone, that is to say, who comes to the front door) *thinks he is a gentleman*. There is a second principle of almost equal importance: *everyone draws the line of demarcation immediately below his own heels*'. This is a typically English version of Field-Marshal Prince Windisch-Grätz's famous crack that *der Mensch beginnt beim Baron*, mankind begins with barons. But there is another aspect, summed up in its negative form in the martial offence of 'conduct un-becoming an officer and a gentleman'. It's positive form should not, in my opinion, simply follow that of the good fairy Do-as-you-would-be-done-by in *The Water Babies*. For this can give *carte blanche* to fanatically self-righteous opinionated do-gooders, upsetting people 'for their own good'. Rather it should be Do-as-they-would-like-to-be-done-by. As Dicky Buckle himself once put it to me, a gentleman should not take pleasure in class distinctions, but should rather seek to ignore them. He should of course lay more emphasis on kindness – for instance, he shouldn't ostentatiously stick to U-shibboleths when drinking with or greeted by non-U speakers who say 'cheers' or 'pleased to meet you', but should try to respond courteously in like manner. Of course it rather goes against the grain.

Of course, too, the nobility and gentry who formed the old aristocracy didn't always live up to their ideals. As Sir George Sitwell pointed out, one of the earliest recorded gents was 'Robert Erdeswyke of Stafford, gentilman', who in 1414 was charged with 'procuring the murder of one Thomas Page, who was cut to pieces while on his knees begging for his life'. But their ideals were there as a shining example all the same. Everybody understands what is, or rather ought to be, meant by one's word of honour as a *gentleman*. Nobody would have accused Hitler or Stalin of being gentlemen. Nor would anybody describe them as noble characters. Yet the word *noble* has so often denoted 'of lofty character or ideals' that that's got into the dictionary as one of its meanings. Of course there's always the danger of the gentleman becoming the genteel man. However, 'truly noble' or 'a perfect gentleman' still mean something less unattractive than 'a complete boor'. *Aristocracy* is from the Greek words 'aristos' meaning 'best' and 'kratia' meaning rule, though the best people can so easily become the Best People. It's of course impossible to have both quality and equality, which latter is the opposite of equality of opportunity. But true quality can stagnate into the Quality. Courtesy – I repeat, the manners of a Court – and Chivalry, the code of the chevaliers, cannot but be a Good Thing, much to be encouraged in the young as one gets older (though note that one shouldn't treat people 'cavalierly' oneself). Though birth counts for less nowadays, most people would still rather behave as though they were 'well-bred' than 'ill-bred'. As we become increasingly classless financially, the English concept that a gentleman is recognised by his code of conduct and manner of life must make it possible for more and more people to be gentlemen because they have chosen to be, and so are.

But don't take all this too seriously. Gents should never appear too keen in public, nor lose their sense of humour. Naturally they are accustomed to excel, but equally to appear to do it with ease and not too openly.

Fine models of gentlemen are to be found in the kindly heroes of P. G. Wodehouse or in the subtle good-humoured concealed character and remarkable but apparently effortless achievements of the Scarlet Pimpernel. For a debonair gentleman – we can alas no longer say a gay, debonair cavalier – so often conceals the skilled professional behind an apparently amateur façade.

Nancy Mitford went in for the occasional quiet tease herself. Her broad thesis was that in U speech a novel French word shouldn't normally be used when an old English one will do, *e.g.* she preferred 'napkin' to 'serviette'. Into the novel French 'refained' category she had wrongly consigned the word mirror, which in fact came over with the Conqueror. When she visited us in Scotland, I pointed out in vain that Shakespeare used the words 'mirror' and 'looking glass' in the same passage. At last, I wrote to her in Paris to play my trump card. My children's ancestral uncle, Sir Alexander Boyd, beheaded in 1469 after kidnapping the boy king, James III while instructing him in knightly exercises, was known to his contemporaries (long before the French governesses of the industrial revolution's *nouveaux riches*) as 'a Mirror of Chivalry'. How was I to describe him to my sons?

She sent back a postcard: "Did they really call him that? How vulgar of them."

Appendix: Our Contributors

As most of the contributors to this volume were persons of some distinction or writers whose work was well known it was thought that, instead of summarizing their careers it might be of interest to show the genealogical connections, if any, between them. If records were kept, and if we delved deep enough into history, we must all prove to be related: the problem is to find the link. A little desultory research was begun without much hope of results.

Certain close cousinships were easily revealed, if not known already. Lord Harewood had a Moncreiffe great-great-grandmother, so he was a fourth cousin of Sir Iain, the present baronet. Mr Sykes was allied to Mr Buckle through the Cavendish-Bentincks and through the Foulises, and to Mr Montague-Smith through the Thynnes; the editor of *Debrett's Peerage* and the editor of the present volume both derived from a seventeenth-century Lord Saye and Sele. But how were those people related to Nancy Mitford and her sisters, one of whom has contributed to this book, or to Professor Ross or to Mr Philip Howard? Had all the contributors one common ancestor and could he be found? It was also a question of space.

Until the present century, when the Royal Family began marrying commoners, the last King of England from whom a non-Royal person could legitimately descend was King Henry VII, who married the Plantagenet heiress. A perusal of Ruvigny's *Blood Royal of Great Britain* proved that most of the contributors, or their wives, descended from the first Tudor monarch. TABLE 1 shows how this happens. It had never been the intention to illustrate Royal descents: it became a convenient way of saving space. (By and large, one can say that the descendants of King Henry's elder daughter Margaret were either Royal or foreign: those of his younger daughter Mary, who had no issue of her first husband, King Louis XII of France, then married Charles Brandon, Duke of Suffolk, were English and non-Royal. It is with the latter that TABLE 1 is concerned.)

TABLE 1 spreads over three pages; the descendants of Lady Frances Brandon, elder daughter of the Duchess of Suffolk, being shown on pages 108–109, those of her sister Lady Eleanor Brandon on page 110. Although the Mitford sisters are the only 'subjects' of the Table whose double descent from King Henry VII is shown, Mrs Philip Howard, Mr Christopher Sykes and Lord Harewood (on his father's side) all have a second descent, which is indicated in the Note on p. 111. On his mother's side Lord Harewood's descents from the Tudor King and his Plantagenet Queen are, of course, more numerous.

In TABLE 2, for reasons of space, it was impossible to show more than the lines of descent, so the names of husbands and wives have been omitted. This Table was made possible because Professor Ross, like most Scots, knew who his ancestors were, even though he kept quiet about them until Richard Buckle dragged the information out of him. It was thus easy for Mr Montague-Smith to show the Professor's cousinship with the late Nancy Mitford, which no doubt would have delighted her as much as it surprised him. Their descent, and that of other contributors, from a Moncrieffe who died in 1496, is carried back six more generations to King Robert the Bruce (1274-1329).

It is much harder to find a non-Royal ancestor for a miscellaneous group of people than to find a Royal one. Although TABLE 3 hardly achieves this, as it only shows a connection between Sir Cecil Beaton and the Mitfords, not a blood relationship, it may still, we hope, prove of particular interest. Also, in contrast to the Tudor, Plantagenet and Scottish descents of the two previous tables, the third illustrates an influx of French Huguenot blood into the British race. This resulted from the Revocation by King Louis XIV of the Edict of Nantes in 1685.

Mr H. B. Brooks-Baker declined to take up space. His Baker ancestors went to America in 1680: through his French wife's mother, a La Rochefoucauld, he is allied to most of the great houses of Europe. His children are descended through the La Rochefoucauld Dukes of Doudeauville and Bisaccia, the Princes of Ligne and Salm and Edward, Prince Palatine, son of Queen Elizabeth of Bohemia, from King James VI and I, Mary, Queen of Scots and King James V of Scotland; and thus from Margaret Tudor, *elder* daughter of King Henry VII.

King Henry VII *m* Elizabeth of York, daughter of King Edward IV

Mary Tudor *m* Charles Brandon, Duke of Suffolk

Lady Frances Brandon *m* Henry Grey, 3rd Marquess of Dorset, Duke of Suffolk

Lady Katherine Grey *m* Edward Seymour, Earl of Hertford

Edward Seymour, Lord Beauchamp *m* Honora Rogers

Francis Seymour, 1st Lord Seymour of Trowbridge
=Frances Prynne

Charles Seymour, 2nd Lord Seymour of Trowbridge *m* Hon. Elizabeth Alington

Charles, 6th Duke of Somerset
=Lady Elizabeth Percy

Algernon Seymour,
7th Duke of Somerset,
Earl of Northumberland
and Egremont   =   Frances Thynne

Hon. Henry Thynne
=Grace Strode

Lady Elizabeth Seymour
=Sir Hugh Smithson,
4th Bt
1st Duke of
Northumberland

Algernon Percy,
1st Earl of Beverley
=Isabella Burrell

Lady Charlotte Percy
=George Ashburnham,
3rd Earl of Ashburnham

Lady Georgiana
Ashburnham
=Henry Reveley-Mitford

Algernon Mitford,
1st Lord Redesdale
=Lady Clementina Ogilvy

David Mitford,
2nd Lord Redesdale
=Sydney Bowles

NANCY
MITFORD
(HON. MRS
RODD)

DIANA
MITFORD
(HON. LADY MOSLEY)

TABLE I Tudor and Plantagenet descents

Descendants of LADY
ELEANOR BRANDON
on next page

William Seymour, 2nd Duke of Somerset *m* Lady Frances Devereux

Lady Mary Seymour =Heneage Finch, 3rd Earl of Winchilsea	Lady Jane Seymour =Charles Boyle, Lord Clifford, Viscount Dungarvan	Henry, Lord Beauchamp =Hon. Mary Capell
Lady Frances Finch =Thomas Thynne, 1st Viscount Weymouth	Charles Boyle, 3rd Earl of Cork, 2nd Earl of Burlington =Juliana Noel	Lady Elizabeth Seymour =Thomas Bruce, 3rd Earl of Elgin and 2nd Earl of Ailesbury
Hon. Frances Thynne =Sir Robert Worsley, 4th Bt	Richard Boyle, 4th Earl of Cork, 3rd Earl of Burlington =Lady Dorothy Savile	Lady Elizabeth Bruce =George Brudenell, 3rd Earl of Cardigan
Frances Worsley =John Carteret, 2nd Earl Granville	Charlotte Boyle, Baroness Clifford =William Cavendish, 4th Duke of Devonshire	George Montagu, 1st Duke of Montague =Lady Mary Montagu
Lady Grace Carteret =Lionel Tollemache, 4th Earl of Dysart	Lady Dorothy Cavendish =William Bentinck, 3rd Duke of Portland	Lady Elizabeth Montagu =Henry Scott, 3rd Duke of Buccleuch and 5th Duke of Queensberry
Lady Jane Tollemache =John Halliday	Lady Charlotte Bentinck =Charles Greville	Lady Caroline Scott = Charles Douglas, 6th Marquess of Queensberry
Charlotte Halliday =Henry Wolseley	Algernon Greville =Charlotte Cox	Lady Louisa Anne Douglas =Thomas Whitmore
William Wolseley =Elizabeth Daniell	Augusta Greville =George Sandford	Thomas Whitmore =Louisa Cradock- Hartopp
Eliza-Jane Wolseley =Rev. John Bourne	Francis Sandford =Constance Craven	Ethel Whitmore =Sir William Houldsworth, 3rd Bt
Wykeham Bourne =Ann Brereton	Rose Sandford =Christopher Buckle	Sir Reginald Houldsworth, 4th Bt =Margaret Laurie
Sybil Bourne =Vernon Montague-Smith	RICHARD BUCKLE	Myrtle Houldsworth =PHILIP HOWARD
PATRICK MONTAGUE-SMITH		

King Henry VII *m* Elizabeth of York, daughter of King Edward IV

Mary Tudor *m* Charles Brandon, Duke of Suffolk

Lady Eleanor Brandon *m* Henry Clifford, 2nd Earl of Cumberland

Lady Margaret Clifford *m* Henry Stanley, 4th Earl of Derby

Ferdinando Stanley,
5th Earl of Derby
=Alice Spencer

Lady Frances Stanley
=John Egerton,
1st Earl of Bridgwater

John Egerton
2nd Earl of Bridgwater
=Lady Elizabeth
Cavendish

Hon. Thomas Egerton
=Hester Busby

John Egerton
=Elizabeth Barbour

Hester Egerton
=William Tatton

Elizabeth Tatton
=Sir Christopher Sykes,
2nd Bt

Sir Tatton Sykes, 3rd Bt
=Mary Ann Foulis

Sir Tatton Sykes, 4th Bt
=Christine Cavendish-
Bentinck

Sir Mark Sykes, 6th Bt
=Edith Gorst

CHRISTOPHER SYKES

William Stanley,
6th Earl of Derby
=Lady Elizabeth Vere

James, 7th Earl of Derby
=Charlotte de
La Tremoille

Lady Amelia Stanley
=John Murray,
1st Marquess of Atholl

Lady Amelia Murray
=Hugh Fraser,
9th Lord Lovat

Hon. Catherine Fraser
=Sir William Murray,
3rd Bt

Catherine Murray
=Sir Thomas Moncreiffe,
3rd Bt

Sir William Moncreiffe,
4th Bt
=Clara Guthrie

Sir Thomas Moncreiffe,
5th Bt
=Lady Elisabeth Ramsay

Sir David Moncreiffe,
6th Bt
=Helen Mackay

Sir Thomas Moncreiffe,
7th Bt
=Lady Louisa Hay

Harry Moncreiffe
=Elisabeth Muir

Gerald Moncreiffe
=Hinda de Miremont

SIR IAIN MONCREIFFE,
11TH BT

Georgina Moncreiffe
=George Bridgeman,
2nd Earl of Bradford

Orlando Bridgeman,
3rd Earl of Bradford
=Hon. Selina Forester

Lady Florence Bridgeman
=Henry Lascelles,
5th Earl of Harewood

Henry Lascelles,
6th Earl of Harewood
=HRH Princess Mary
of Great Britain,
Princess Royal

GEORGE LASCELLES,
7TH EARL OF HAREWOOD

TABLE I
Tudor and
Plantagenet
descents

Two descents of the Mitford sisters from King Henry VII have been shown. Other 'subjects' of this Table also have two descents, which have been omitted because of typographical difficulties. Christopher Sykes's paternal grandmother, Christine Cavendish-Bentinck, was great-granddaughter of the 3rd Duke of Portland, who occurs on p. 110, so he is descended from Lady Frances Brandon as well as Lady Eleanor Brandon. Myrtle (Houldsworth) Howard's great-great-great-grandfather, the 3rd Duke of Buccleuch and 5th Duke of Queensberry, was great-great-grandson of Lady Jane Seymour and Viscount Dungarvan, so that he, as well as his wife, were descended from King Henry VII (and, incidentally from the Protector Somerset). Lord Harewood's great-great-grandmother, Lady Louisa Thynne, wife of the 3rd Earl, was descended through the (Torrington) Byngs, (Cork) Boyles and (Exeter) Cecils from Lady Frances Stanley, wife of John Egerton, 1st Earl of Bridgwater, who is shown as one of Christopher Sykes's links with the Tudors and Plantagenets.

As stated on p. 107, Lord Harewood, is descended through his Royal mother a number of times from King Henry VII, but we have not considered it necessary to illustate these descents. (A moment's thought will reveal that the cousinship of King George V and Queen Mary – both descended from King George III – would give two descents; while that of Mary, Queen of Scots, and her consort Lord Darnley would give two more: but that is only the beginning of the story.)

King Robert the Bruce
= (1) Isabella, dau. of the Earl of Mar[1]
= (2) Elizabeth de Burgh, dau. of 2nd Earl of Ulster

Lady Maud Bruce

Joan de Ysak

Isobel MacDougall

Christian Stewart

Beatrix Dundas

John Moncreiffe, 8th of that Ilk, *d* 1496

	Margaret Moncreiffe[3]
Hew Moncreiffe[2]	Catherine Campbell
	Sir William Murray of Tullibardine
Descent of SIR IAIN MONCREIFFE and the EARL OF HAREWOOD	Sir John Murray, 1st Earl of Tullibardine

Lady Anne Murray

John Lyon, 2nd Earl of Kinghorne

Patrick Lyon, 3rd Earl of Strathmore
and Kinghorne

John Lyon,
4th Earl of Strathmore

Thomas Lyon,
8th Earl of Strathmore

Lady Anne Lyon[4]

Maria Simpson

Hon. Susan Liddell

Lady Mary Yorke

Constance Craven

Rose Sandford

RICHARD BUCKLE

This table, compiled by Patrick Montague-Smith, illustrates only the lines of descent, husbands and wives being omitted.

[1] From the first marriage of King Robert I to Isabella, daughter of the Earl of Mar, descend the Stewart (or Stuart) Kings of Scotland and England, and, through Queen Elizabeth of Bohemia, daughter of King James VI and I, the present Royal House.

[2] From Hew Moncreiffe, Sir Thomas Moncreiffe, 5th Bart., shown on TABLE I, was 8th in descent. (Sir Ian Moncreiffe of that Ilk, 11th Bart., is descended over 600 times from Robert the Bruce.)

[3] Margaret Moncreiffe and her sister Agnes married half-brothers, Sir Duncan Campbell, 2nd of Glenorchy; and Sir John Campbell of Lawers.

[4] From Lady Anne Lyon's brother John Lyon, 9th Earl of Strathmore and his wife Mary, heiress of George Bowes, descend subsequent Earls of Strathmore and HM The Queen Mother.

[5] Professor Ross believes that his great-great-great-grandfather John Clark, the husband of Helen Campbell, was descended from a Cameron of Lochiel who changed his name to Clark after taking part in the '45 rebellion.

Agnes Moncreiffe[3]

John Campbell of Murthly

Margaret Murray

John Campbell of
Edramuckie and Kenknock

Col. Norman Bruce

Katherine Bruce

Patrick Campbell of
Easter Shian

Elizabeth Murray,
Countess of Dysart

John Campbell of Easter
Shian and Easter Garrows

Lionel Tollemache,
3rd Earl of Dysart

Patrick Campbell of
Easter Shian and
Easter Garrows

Lady Grizel Lyon

Lionel Tollemache,
Lord Huntingtower

John Ogilvy,
5th Earl of Airlie

Lionel Tollemache,
4th Earl of Dysart

William Campbell

Walter Ogilvy,
8th Earl of Airlie

Helen Campbell[5]

David Ogilvy,
9th Earl of Airlie

Mary Clark

See TABLE I for
descent of
PATRICK MONTAGUE-
SMITH

Archibald Colquhoun Ross

David Ogilvy,
10th Earl of Airlie

Charles Campbell Ross

Lady Clementina Ogilvy

Archibald Campbell
Carne Ross

David Mitford,
2nd Lord Redesdale

PROFESSOR ALAN S. C. ROSS

NANCY MITFORD   DIANA MITFORD

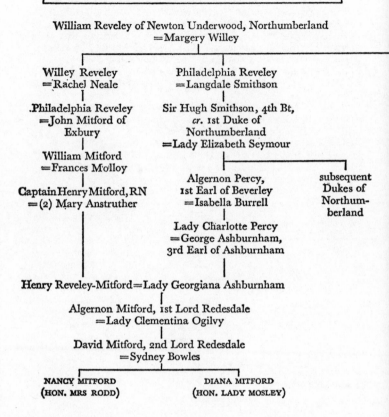

TABLE 3 The Beaton connection. Reveley and Champion de Crespigny (Huguenot) descents.

William Reveley of Newton Underwood, Northumberland
=Margery Willey

Willey Reveley
=Rachel Neale

Philadelphia Reveley
=John Mitford of
Exbury

William Mitford
=Frances Molloy

Captain Henry Mitford, RN
=(2) Mary Anstruther

Philadelphia Reveley
=Langdale Smithson

Sir Hugh Smithson, 4th Bt,
cr. 1st Duke of
Northumberland
=Lady Elizabeth Seymour

Algernon Percy,
1st Earl of Beverley
=Isabella Burrell

subsequent
Dukes of
Northum-
berland

Lady Charlotte Percy
=George Ashburnham,
3rd Earl of Ashburnham

Henry Reveley-Mitford=Lady Georgiana Ashburnham

Algernon Mitford, 1st Lord Redesdale
=Lady Clementina Ogilvy

David Mitford, 2nd Lord Redesdale
=Sydney Bowles

NANCY MITFORD
(HON. MRS RODD)

DIANA MITFORD
(HON. LADY MOSLEY)

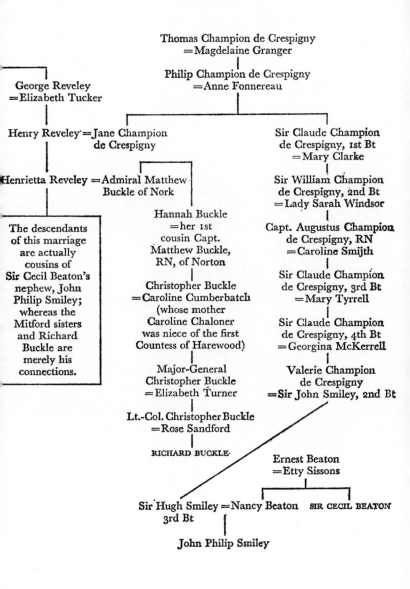

Thomas Champion de Crespigny
=Magdelaine Granger

Philip Champion de Crespigny
=Anne Fonnereau

George Reveley
=Elizabeth Tucker

Henry Reveley=Jane Champion
de Crespigny

Sir Claude Champion
de Crespigny, 1st Bt
=Mary Clarke

Henrietta Reveley =Admiral Matthew
Buckle of Nork

Sir William Champion
de Crespigny, 2nd Bt
=Lady Sarah Windsor

The descendants
of this marriage
are actually
cousins of
Sir Cecil Beaton's
nephew, John
Philip Smiley;
whereas the
Mitford sisters
and Richard
Buckle are
merely his
connections.

Hannah Buckle
=her 1st
cousin Capt.
Matthew Buckle,
RN, of Norton

Capt. Augustus Champion
de Crespigny, RN
=Caroline Smijth

Christopher Buckle
=Caroline Cumberbatch
(whose mother
Caroline Chaloner
was niece of the first
Countess of Harewood)

Sir Claude Champion
de Crespigny, 3rd Bt
=Mary Tyrrell

Sir Claude Champion
de Crespigny, 4th Bt
=Georgina McKerrell

Major-General
Christopher Buckle
=Elizabeth Turner

Valerie Champion
de Crespigny
=Sir John Smiley, 2nd Bt

Lt.-Col. Christopher Buckle
=Rose Sandford

RICHARD BUCKLE

Ernest Beaton
=Etty Sissons

Sir Hugh Smiley =Nancy Beaton   SIR CECIL BEATON
3rd Bt

John Philip Smiley

"How vulgar of them."